OAXACA
Stories Along the Way

More by James E. Gaasch

Diversité, La Nouvelle francophone (edited with Valérie Budig); *Anthologie de la nouvelle maghrébine; La Nouvelle Sénégalaise Texte et Contexte; African Masks of Burkina Faso and Mali A Trilingual Edition, and Oaxaca and Beyond Bilingual Microstories From The Heart* (as a writer and editor with Rosamel S. Benavides-Garb, and as an editor with Rolando Fernando Martínez Sánchez and Francisco Ruiz Cervantes).

Cover art: "In The Shade Of A Pomegranate Tree" by Judith Romero: *This was the scene of a conversation with J, A and H on the patio of the Oaxacan restaurant El Cabuche. H is usually alone at this table, sheltered only by a white pomegranate tree.*

OAXACA
STORIES ALONG THE WAY

A NOVELLA BY
JAMES E. GAASCH

THE PRESS AT CAL POLY HUMBOLDT

Cover art: "In The Shade Of A Pomegranate Tree" by Judith Romero: *This was the scene of a conversation with J, A and H on the patio of the Oaxacan restaurant El Cabuche. H is usually alone at this table, sheltered only by a white pomegranate tree.*

The photo for the bio was taken by Craig C. Stein

Cover design by Wilder Yaconelli
Typesetting and layout by Wilder Yaconelli
Editing by Dorothy Pendleton and Wilder Yaconelli

©2025 James E. Gaasch
The Press at Cal Poly Humboldt
California State Polytechnic University, Humboldt
University Library
1 Harpst Street
Arcata, California 95521-8299
press@humboldt.edu
press.humboldt.edu

Hardcover ISBN: 978-1-962081-27-6
Paperback ISBN: 978-1-962081-26-9

Text set in Adobe Aldine
Chapter headers: Centaur
Cover Text: Baskerville Old Face

For Micaela, Siena Violet, Sawyer, Solana
and Adrian

CONTENTS

"Ninguna aventura de la imaginación tiene más valor literario que el más insignificante episodio de la vida cotidiana." -Gabriel García Márquez

"No adventure of the imagination has more literary value than the most insignifcant episode of daily life." -Gabriel García Márquez

"Mi trabajo casi siempre parte de situaciones autobiográficas, a veces también desde los desplazamientos... puede haber una relación con la obra de Muybridge [Eadweard Muybridge]... en mi caso, en torno al desplazamiento territorial y espacial, así como a la relación de éstos con las situaciones históricas y políticas que vamos viviendo." -Selma Guisande

"My work almost always starts from autobiographical situations, sometimes also from displacements... there may be a relationship with Muybridge's [Eadweard Muybridge] work ... in my case about territorial and spacial displacement, and their relationship to historical and political situations we live through. -Selma Guisande

PROLOGUE

Who is H? This question is the point of entry for the curious reader who seeks a narrative identity. Possibly, this very quest may also be a seductive trap, for it may not matter who H really is, but rather how he travels in multiple directions, geographically, intellectually, and spiritually through the fraught, yet real and fictional landscape of Oaxaca. H first appears in another literary work in *Oaxaca and Beyond*, a short story anthology dedicated to Oaxaca. The short story, "Transitions in Oaxaca" penned by James Ephraim Gaasch is about H's visit to the opening of an art exhibit in Oaxaca. In many ways, this short story announces the novella *OAXACA: Stories Along the Way*, and is the novella's first story.

H is the central character who weaves together the stories of this novella as a narrator, interlocutor and ethnographer, while observing a complex historical, social, and human moment. In this process he takes notes about what he sees and hears. Within these pages, H regularly translates from Spanish to English and at times from French to English. It appears that what we are presently reading are the random jottings in H's notebook.

Yes, along the way, accompanying H, we interrogate the past, present, and future of individuals who are part of the mestizo and indigenous communities of this remote and culturally rich region of southern Mexico. In this journey, we also have a chance to learn of the Black communities of Mexico as well, a surprise for some readers, yet just another poignant and invisible truth of Mexico.

The reader, along with H, encounters ordinary people with extraordinary stories or is it the other way around? However, it would be prudent to warn the reader that there are a few monsters along the way, for example, the "collective shadow" mentioned in the first story. A conversation in the streets of Oaxaca, a mural or graffiti, a gathering at an art gallery, urgent e-mails from Africa, a conversation with a friend, or a visit to an ancient cave may linger for a very long time in the reader's imagination, in the same way they have lingered in the imagination of H. Would it be more accurate to say that these scenes will linger in the "memory" of the reader? For the people and places of this novella will dwell in the memory of the reader as a personal experience. In addition, our old friend, Don Quixote, may manifest in this journey in unexpected ways. Fiction and reality may well be part of the same continuum. Real lived experience and imagination inhabit the present.

The reader has the option to organize the novella in a coherent sequence of stories with intentional or implicit connections, or may choose to see the work as independent stories, vignettes that take place in Oaxaca. In both cases, H is a patient and insightful observer who guides us to people, history, places, and spaces.

The story is also told from the perspective of a main narrator who facilitates H's journey through Oaxaca. This narrator emerges slowly as an intriguing voice who at times asks questions regarding the matters observed as if encountering them, like H, for the first time. Often this narrator may dissolve itself within the essence of H or vice versa. These points of intersection may challenge the traditional way we have understood the voice and role of a third person, the omniscient narrator. Understanding this hybrid narrator may present another hint to better appreciate the architecture of the entire work.

I should not omit a significant stroke of structural and intentional intertextuality deployed in this novella because it may provide a unique dimension of Gaasch as a master writer. The reader may not know that the Oaxaca anthology mentioned above, where H was first introduced in "Oaxacan Transitions," featured an exceptional book cover, a picture of now famous Aunt Chona, an Afro Mexican descendent from the town of Valerio Trujano. This photograph was taken by the prominent photojournalist Judith Romero. All this comes into the novella in several ways, creating a circular design, internal and external. The photo subtly bridges two literary works. There is continuity at the fictional and real levels, a perfect circle, impossible to reduce to a gaming theory.

I leave many reading clues pending, like hidden sounds in an ancient cave, for the reader to discover them. Yes, there is more to this seemingly unassuming novella. I am inviting the reader to come along and journey with me to complete this prologue, for reading is always an adventure.

James Ephraim Gaasch has successfully crafted an ingenious, yet self-effacing literary work which reveals a cultural and emotional map where we are invited to locate ourselves too. This should be said carefully as the architecture, the way and manner the story is laid in front of us, presents a few challenges to the reader. Is this story a testimonial novella, a realistic novella or a purely fictional exercise, a game of sorts? Is Gaasch questioning our traditional narrative schemes as insufficient to tell what he wants to tell? I'll let the reader ponder this matter, but be ready to be surprised. This novella may be many things for different readers, and, as we follow H down the path, we may well end up discovering hidden dimensions of ourselves along the way.

Rosamel Segundo Benavides-Garb
Arcata, California

TRANSITIONS IN OAXACA

H had been looking forward to the afternoon of the ninth. M had invited him to the opening of the exhibition, Dialogue on the Gallop, that would feature works by a Mexican visual artist and the English photographer Eadweard Muybridge. Opening night of the event was at the Centro Fotográfico Manuel Álvarez Bravo. H arrived late. M had already spoken and introduced S. H crossed the threshold, stepped into the Moorish courtyard, and met the calming presence of still, reflective water.

A century and a half earlier in San Francisco, Muybridge had been engaged by Leland Stanford, the North American railroad baron, to settle a wager with a friend. A galloping horse's hooves are, at one point, completely in the air, Stanford contended. As it turned out, Stanford won the bet thanks to Muybridge's use of multiple cameras and lenses that captured, at precise moments, the horse's flying hooves.

M, an international journalist, rests at water's edge, speaking too softly for H to hear well. It has been decades. M hasn't changed. Two women guests lean into M's words, muffling all but fragments:

"We're here this afternoon... Well, it's the word 'sombra,' dark, that .... You know what I mean ... for this exhibit . . . that won't be tonight's story. The back-story doesn't pertain.... What counts now is S's work, and these two artists."

H turns to his left. Two smartly dressed women speak, pressed at his elbow:

"R and K aren't here."

"No. R was stung by black wasps a few days ago and was laid low by the attack. Weird, no?"

"You know how upset R was when he heard of this —you know what I mean— what happened to S. He's a sensitive man."

"Why, oh why, is there so much violence these days? So much pain for so many people."

"I heard M say that violence always seems to be here in Mexico, a kind of 'sombra colectiva,' a dark hangover from the Conquest."

"And all our long internal violence -- independence and revolution -- and to Mexican women."

"Are you sure that M said that?"

"Yes, he said that! A man can be right, too, no?"

"I think that we'd better go look at S's works now, don't you? It's getting crowded."

H moves on; he wants to speak with A about a current project, but his way is blocked. Known for his writings on Mexican social history, A holds forth, surrounded by ardent listeners. H can't hear everything A is is saying, but knows it's about J and her photography, probably her documentation on Afro-Mexican women:

"Sure, J's work is related to S's art. J has been exploring from a feminist perspective the decisions women make. I mean the decisions they're forced to make, living within their cultural constraints. Her photographs, ... Her interviews with indigenous women.... Taboos.... Those forced decisions that women confront."

A turns his back, and H can no longer hear him. J is standing next to H now, speaking softly, almost whispering to him:

"A would like to speak with you, H. Why don't you interrupt him?"

"Oh, I wouldn't feel comfortable doing that. I'll just talk to him another time. What have you been doing, J?"

"Well, I'm excited; I've been invited to film the making of a movie in Sierra Sur. But I'll tell you more about it, when I get back in a few weeks."

Before H leaves the Centro Fotográfico, he pauses to stand in front of Transition, S's large ceramic piece: Maybe, he reflects, this is where S and Muybridge share another creative moment.

Naked, anonymous, glazed white against a backdrop of black, a man steps over a red pool and appears ready to ascend distant stairs. Stopped (only momentarily?), the man may be moving toward something. Towards what? Extraordinary in what is commonplace: a fragile narrative, suspended at a precise moment. S's gaze: white, black and red shards of a masculine world.

H leaves the Centro and returns to his hotel, just a few blocks away. There, after two shots of mezcal, through a fog of alcohol, H listens to the audio that M sent him, his interview with S. First, S responds to M's question about Muybridge's use of sequential images and his artistic vision of impermanence:

"The reason that I'd been working with photographs of Muybridge and other photographers is because I was really investigating memory and our collective shadow."

Here there's silence. A break in the audio? H fumbles, drops his sharpened pencil. The audio continues, H stoops over and, finally, on hands and knees under his desk, gropes hard for something pointed. He can't find it. From under the desk, he grasps for words, any bits and pieces of what S is saying. H, caught tight, boxed in, imagines he's still scribbling, even feeling the words, their fabric. Yes. He's getting something! S is answering:

"Time becomes dysphasic.... The asymmetry of my work... an intuitive process... an endless series of hair diaries...

like a loop, back and forth between the real object and its representation... open up possibilities for new readings... almost always starts from the autobiographical... but very whimsical, as well... there is a response to anthropocentrism, to patriarchy."

Alone, maybe hours later, naked, legs stretched out from under his desk, H sleeps — an amber slumber.

The solace of mezcal, more shots, warms the room. The audio has stopped. Pages spent, ripped from their catalogue binding; the remains of Dialogue on the Gallop lie close by.

Uncounted hours. H awakens. Bits and pieces of S's words, neatly cut paper rectangles, cling high to the dark wall, sharp scissors nearby.

Days later, H returns to the Centro Fotográfico to look again at S's work. But at this midmorning hour on a Monday, school kids in blue uniforms and multicolored aprons occupy all the exhibit rooms. Their teachers walk from table to table, smiling and commenting. These kids, maybe ten years old, draw and copy the figures they see in ceramic, paper and plastic, the animals and humans in locomotion. H moves among them unnoticed. Each child has captured, created a version of the works of S and Muybridge. Some of their pages are almost blank; some are filled, edge to edge, with different renderings of the same piece. One kid, staring at S's Transition, has drawn a solitary stick figure, limbs outstretched in suspended motion.

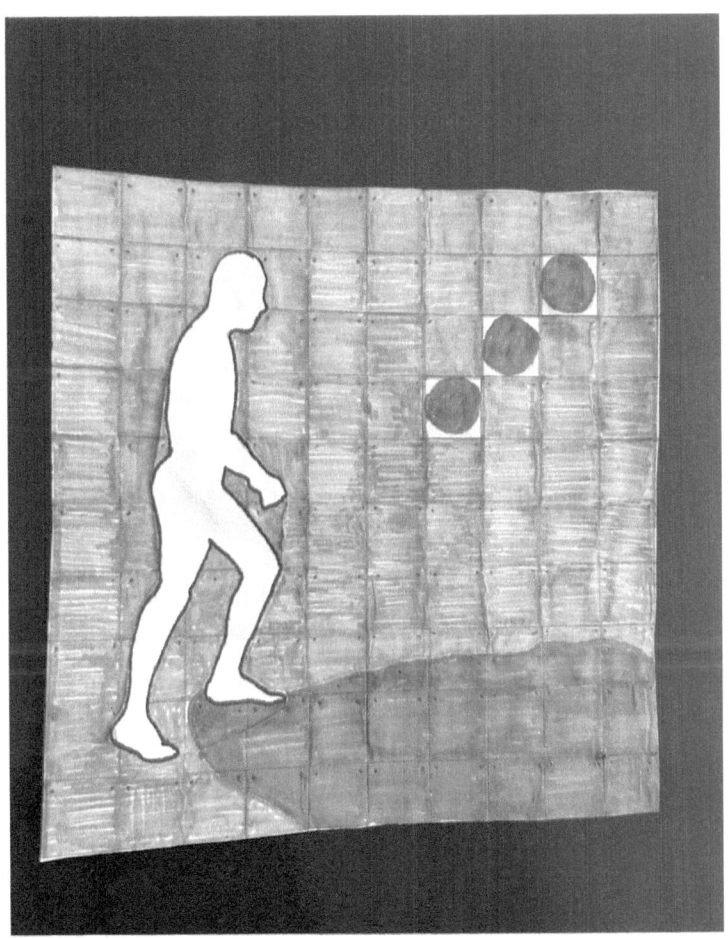

Transition by Selma Guisande

Days after the opening night for the exhibition, Dialogue on the Gallop, at the Centro Fotográfico Manuel Bravo, H watches school children draw, after a fashion, the hanging ceramic piece of art, Transition, by Selma Guisande. Above, the pencil drawn rendition of Transition sketched by Q.

Back in Oaxaca

In Oaxaca, after a hiatus of several months, H, a solitary man, a creature of habits and obsessions, writes or rewrites during the same hours every morning — in fruitless search of le mot juste. His plan now is to write while spending a few months in Oaxaca; he'll live out of a suitcase until his latest edited book, *Oaxaca and Beyond, Bilingual Microstories From the Heart*, is launched by the university here and is on the shelves of Oaxaca's bookstores. Making the anthology available in local bookstores will be the real challenge; the university has—perhaps undeserved—the reputation for publishing books and only sharing them with a few colleagues and friends and then storing them for an eternity in a warehouse with long-forgotten stacks of such publications.

With the collaboration of two Mexican academic editors and an American-Chilean close friend and colleague, H has worked for the last eighteen months with fourteen Mexican writers on an anthology of bilingual short stories. The process has been rewarding, forming new and lasting friendships— but not without its moments of frustration. He has lived with the sensibilities, sensibilities often à fleur de peau, of Oaxacan short story writers, all good writers who believe in the power of literature, among them Guadalupe Ángela, Manuel Matus Manzo, Antonio Pacheco Zárate, Gayne Rodríguez Guzmán, Jessica Santiago Guzmán, Cuauhtémoc Peña Vásquez and more. H is aware that being in Oaxaca during these months is a privilege. Creative energy flourishes here: graphic artists, photographers, writers are the city's bone and sinew; art on the buildings and in galeries; book launchings—readings and signings in the many bookstores and other urban spaces.

Reading books of Oaxacan short stories has nourished H's waking hours, days on end. Of course, reading, walking and friends are essential parts of his life no matter where he happens to be. But the intensity of the creative spirit of Oaxaca has a way of molding his habits and obsessions to its own time. Although suffering from insomnia the first nights, he's soon focused in the mornings; it's the best time to write, best with a cup or two of coffee, with no food—later, breakfast... and then a long walk. Once he finds his footing, he knows the first days will be grand: in the street—he hears new languages, feels a palpable energy, a moving strangeness. "Yes, being back in Oaxaca will be fine, for a while," he thinks aloud to himself.

In H's suitcase are tattered paperbacks; Miguel de Unamuno and Claude Lévi-Strauss are his constant, uncomplaining companions. But for grins, he's been reading a book, he bought on his last trip at Amate bookstore—or was it at Caleidoscopio?—*The Guilty*, collection of short stories by the Mexican writer, Juan Villoro. Villoro's finely chiseled sentences help H remember the power of biting sarcasm; he feels a kinship with this author. His stories, even in blue evening hours when H is tired, lift his spirits. Villoro's central character, Samuel Katzenberg, is an-almost-sympathetic figure—but in the end Katzenberg remains a journalist forever grasping for fame, cheating, and plagiarizing his way through articles for a well-known New York magazine.

In the short story, "Amigos Mexicanos," Katzenberg is on assignment in Mexico. To help him write his article, he will urgently seek out the story's main character and narrator in Mexico City. Naturally, before leaving the U.S., Katzenberg has consulted his academic sources, professors of cultural study programs in the most prestigious American universities. He knows that he must take with him to Mexico all the tools he will need in order to write the article once there. He knows beforehand that finding the true Mexico will not be easy. For him, the search for authenticity in Mexico, inevitably, logically, means doing an article on Frida Kahlo—while at the same time emphasizing the rampant violence in today's Mexico. For a fee, Villoro's narrator, who is also a screen writer, will oblige Katzenberg and will furnish him with all the clichés, all the tripe that he can invent about Mexico— without ever quenching Katzenberg's enormous appetite for what the journalist perceives to be the real Mexico. Smiling at Villoro's irony, H takes note of Katzenberg's quest and recalls the many imposed and prefabricated cultural stereotypes of Mexico coming from the north, from the U.S.

Leather shoes—*some waiting on a ledge, some taken from E's leather satchel—in a line next to E's stall. It's early morning and the sun warms the leather, making it supple and receptive to E's polishes. Faithful customers return to reclaim their shoes in the late afternoon. Each pair of polished shoes costs 30 pesos, or about $1.50 American.*

THE FEEL OF LEATHER

H awakens early on his first Saturday back on Calle Pino Suárez. Despite a restless night, he's optimistic and decides not to write for a while; instead, after coffee, he'll walk to his favorite tree, a beach sheoak in Conzatti Park where he'll do exercises under the tree's pine-needle-like branches. Anticipating already how it will feel to lean hard for balance into the tall tree's dark, hospitable bark, H quickens his pace as he nears the small park. (When in Southern Oregon, he does the same exercises next to a Blue Atlas Cedar, only a few steps away from a copse of Coastal Redwoods. There, as in Oaxaca, the morning sky seems high and limitless.) When he leaves Conzatti, it's still early in Oaxaca, but H knows he'll likely find E, a Mazatecan Oaxacan, a bootblack, un lustrador de calzados, on a corner of the city's plaza, El Zócalo. His short walk is not in vain: Rows and piles of scuffed black and brown shoes rest neatly on the cement ledge, under the shade of the pollution-stained awning of E's work stall. Left on the sidewalk by faithful customers, the shoes are a sure sign that E is there, or about to arrive.

In past years, E never extended an audible greeting when he first saw H. Even after months of absence, E would acknowledge H's presence only by shifting slightly, almost imperceptibly, on the cushion of his low chair. On this occasion, however, E extracts his right hand from a brown shoe and cordially signals passage to the high seat. Perhaps a conversation will ensue.

"Are you free, Don E(nrique)?" H asks.

"Yes, of course, I can finish these other shoes later." And E gestures to H to take his place on the red vinyl seat.

15

E, fifty-four years old, a slight man about five feet six inches tall, with brown, thinning hair and dark coffee-colored eyes, has occupied this space for more than forty years. To learn his trade, when he was eight, he apprenticed to his older brother. He had been with him less than a year, when the brother was killed in a bus accident while returning to Oaxaca from his hometown, Huautla de Jiménez, in The Sierra Mazateca. Fifteen other passengers perished in the same accident.

For the next two years, E plied the streets of Oaxaca, polishing shoes from a box of waxes, liquids, brushes, and rags, hanging from his shoulder. Then, finally, almost eleven by this time, he was eligible to join a union, gaining the right to work from his own *silla*, his own seat. These days he pays monthly union dues of ten pesos. He awakens at 5am and usually works until 9 in the evening, with coffee and food breaks. "I have no savings plan. I won't be eligible for social security either," he told H. "On weekends, I work as a waiter for events in a local church; I do okay with tips." At home, E is by himself with no company. "I have no friends who come to see me, no friends here or in Huautla de Jiménez, no television, no radio." He and his ex-wife don't see one another, nor does he see his grown son. Over months of interrupted conversations, during H's many stays in Oaxaca, E has shared parts of his life with H.

H has also shared some of his life with E, in the measure that one might expect of H—recounting a little of his life in California on Alcalde Ranch. H must have thought that E might be interested in a solitary child on a remote ranch; H had no childhood friends and didn't start school until he was almost eight. "Do you miss the mountains, the high country of La Sierra Mazateca, E?" H asks, talking over the unrelenting street noise that renders conversation almost impossible on congested streets of Oaxaca. "When I'm in the city," H continues, "I often think of the mountains and the ranch, the California Coastal Range Mountains—Juniper Ridge and Bald Mountain—and of the wild animals, especially the deer, an occasional mountain lion, and the plentiful quail that I would see on horseback with my dad." (H had stopped himself here, thinking that on other occasions he might say more to E; he might talk to E about riding in the back country, looking for stray cattle hiding in thick chaparral, or about riding in Oak Flats, a valley of live oak trees that once belonged to Indians, maybe the Salinan people. Trees, weighted heavily with acorns, dotted this valley, offering sheltering cover to the occasional grinding stone—mano and deep basin metate. H thought that E would understand the feelings that these images evoked, but he never found the moment to talk more about this valley of oak trees and of the high mountains.)

"Yes, I think about the mountains of La Tierra Mazateca," E answers. "They are beautiful around Huautla de Jiménez. My town sits low surrounded by forests and mountains with blue skies above, always blue. I'm not able to visit much, maybe once a year. It's a long bus ride, ten hours. I can't leave my work, and the road past the town of Cuicatlán has many curves; people, kids especially, always get sick on the bus." Listening to E pronounce again the name Huautla de Jiménez, H wonders if he knows the relatives of the famous curandera, María Sabina. H has heard that her relatives, maybe her grandchildren, still reside in E's town. Did María Sabina, la sabia de los hongos, pass on to them her knowledge of the magic mushrooms? Do these relatives still speak el lenguaje chamánico—the language of the shamans of the Mazatecan Country?

At this moment, as E is applying another layer of polish to H's shoes, a man about E's age passes by. E greets him in Mazateco.

"Do you know him ... a friend?" H asks.

"No, he's not a friend of mine, but he speaks Mazateco."

"How did you know that he would speak Mazateco?"

"I could tell ... the way he walked."

H is still feeling the resonance of these words, palabras sueltas, sílabas—remarkable Mazateco sounds—when E nods to another passerby, a well-dressed man. "He's a retired maestro," E says, "a teacher, but not a customer; I don't take care of his shoes." Then turning back, again facing H, E touches his elbow to indicate that the gentleman is a skinflint.

"Well, he's wearing a good pair of leather shoes," H quips. "Everyone these days wears crappy tennis shoes or rubber clogs of one sort or another; the beaches of the world and our landfills are lousy with them." On a roll, H continues, "You can tell, E, by those shoes, teachers in Oaxaca have a good union; teachers everywhere deserve to have a union; their work is hard and important." E looks as though he might agree with what H is saying. H changes the subject, "There are more migrants than usual moving through the Zócalo this morning. It's hard to know where they're all from, but probably from many countries: Guatemala, Honduras, Venezuela, Columbia, Ecuador, Cuba, Haiti and beyond. Even from Africa and China? These places are in the news." H often buys one of the two newspapers, El Imparcial or La Reforma from E's stand. "More and more desperate people. Are they looking for work in Oaxaca, or only headed north, E?"

"Most of them will not stop here to look for work. If they did, they could find work. But they want to earn more money, so they move on. Young people from here also want to go north for the same reason. If they stayed, there's work here for them, too, not as bootblacks; no, young people are ashamed of being bootblacks. In the past, we were many in the park."

"It's the weekend, will you go home early tonight?" H asks.

"No, there's nothing at home for me; I'll stay late."

"Do you know all of the other bootblacks who work in the Zócalo, or the other parks?"

"Yes, I know some of them, some by name. They know me; they call me El Güero, my nickname."

"Güero, in Mexico means someone with light skin or hair, right?"

"Yes, they think that my skin is light ... I really don't like the name; I don't take it as an insult, but I don't like being called out that way."

Remembering that E has been divorced for almost three years, H asks, "You told me that you were married for many years, why separate after living together that long?"

"We never spoke to one another; there was never a connection."

"But did you speak the same language, E?"

E is not quick to respond; then, finally, "No, my wife spoke the language Chinanteco; she didn't speak Mazateco like me. When we talked, it was only in Spanish."

"Did you think of learning some words in Chinanteco to speak with your wife?"

"No, I never thought of that. Maybe that was the problem, nothing in common."

Another long pause, H was thinking what he could say that might offer some comfort. Could he say anything that wouldn't sound hollow? "It must get lonely," H finally hazarded; he could feel E's worn finishing cloth press into the leather of his shoe. H continued, "I'm sometimes lonely at night, after dinner; when I'm too tired to walk or to read, I miss having someone to talk with."

"Yes," here there's a catch in E's throat, "I get lonely some nights." His concentration fixes on H's shoes. "But then I think of my work, the work that I have the next morning, and I feel okay; that helps me. I also think of the company of women."

"A relationship?"

"No. Women aren't interested in me, not in a bootblack; I don't have money to invite them out.

A Red Vinyl Seat

E wheels his seat to the same spot every morning and pushes it out of the main plaza late every night. For the years that H can remember, it has had an uncomfortable cushion. He has been tempted to call this to E's attention. But, of course, once seated and talking to E, H forgets this concern.

FRIENDS & RESTAURANTS

The first days in Oaxaca go by quickly for H. He eats out with old friends, most often with M and C. M is a journalist, now semi-retired, who with his late wife, Margaret, a well-known writer on Mexican photography and women artists in general, accumulated an impressive collection of photography. And when she is free, C joins them. C is a voracious reader and longtime editor in both Mexico and London. She, however, is not often free; she is one of the volunteers handing out warm meals to hundreds of migrants, hungry and exhausted, arriving daily on the streets of Oaxaca. H heard that the meals are prepared for them in a small kitchen close to Jardín Morelos.

H is early for his lunch with M and C. He had remembered to make a reservation at the restaurant El Cabuche, knowing that it would be busy on a Friday afternoon. In fact, there is always a steady flow of tourists on Calle Miguel Hidalgo, where El Cabuche is located. Now, he wonders if, as usual, M and C will arrive late; no matter, he reassures himself, there'll be plenty of time to catch up with one another. In the meantime, the new server (many old faces have been replaced since Covid) seats H at his favorite table, on the north side of the restaurant's intimate patio. When he's by himself, H always chooses this table, perfect for eavesdropping on the patio's conversations. El Cabuche is especially favored by citizens from the vast Spanish speaking world—from Spain to the far reaches of Argentina. Although he doesn't always hear complete sentences (H doesn't hear as well as he used to), he takes solace in playing a guessing game. His guesses often prove accurate as the vowels and consonants and syllables accumulate from across the patio; his ability to identify the language is about speed (tempo) and clarity of pronunciation, H says to himself. The overheard accents, most often from Mexico City, or from Oaxaca's capital or, less often, from Madrid or Barcelona or other regions of Spain, create a natural ebb and flow of sounds, islands of consolation in H's world. It's a very good time to be in Oaxaca.

But this particular restaurant and table are also dear to him because it's where H had a long conversation, months ago, with A and J. Frustrated then, H was at an impasse in his writing of "Transitions In Oaxaca," and needed to ask A about what he had said on the subject of Mexican women weeks earlier during the reception for Dialogue on the Gallop. H had overheard A's barely audible utterances—palabras sueltas, single words adrift. "Just look," A had said—in an ex-cathedra tone. "Look at the book I gave you. I was saying exactly what I wrote." As H listened intently to A, trying to jog his memory of the book, he began to scribble down the title of A's essay and, at the same time, to write the title of the book in which it appears. "Nothing more, nothing less; it's what I wrote about J; that's what I said that evening, H," A finished with a flurry of words and strong conviction. And H knew that he would need to go back to look at the book *Modernity as Labyrinth*.

J, seated close to H, had listened patiently, in apparent agreement with A. H followed assiduously what A was saying, all the while writing in his frayed, all-weather-pocket notebook. Then, smiling (at H's plodding), J abruptly reached for H's notebook and completed his sentences herself. Amused, H remembered liking J's confidence.

As was predictable, before leaving the table, A had recommended yet another book to H: *Streets, Bedrooms & Patios, The Ordinariness of Diversity in Urban Oaxaca* by Michael Higgins and Tanya L. Coen. And, just as predictably,

H had written the long title down. A is a generous scholar—one of the few in the wider academic world that H knew—who had only praise for his colleagues.

H is still lost in memories of that afternoon lunch with J and A when M and C arrive at his table. They are all famished and order straight away the menu of the day: Ensalada criolla (arúgula, toronja, rábano, aguacate, vinagre de Jamaica) and, as the main dish, camarones al pastor (camarones con achiote con piña), followed by arroz con leche for dessert. Although El Cabuche is known for its succulent shrimp dishes, at this moment, with his dark beer, Modelo Negra, H could have easily passed on the rest of the meal.

First turning to M, H asks, "So, what are you up to these days, back in Mexico after all these years? And here in Oaxaca, no less?" The "here in Oaxaca" was meant to elicit current information about Oaxcaca; H knew that M and C were more in step with happenings in Oaxaca than he was. "Is there a lot going on, M?"

"Well, yes, a juggling act, you know, a variety of tasks, projects. In part, I'm dealing with what Margaret gave us, which for a writer primarily involves her work. But also trying to rescue bits and pieces of life that are fragmented, obscured, like when she was political, a women's rights activist in Australia in the 70s, before she became a writer."

"No easy task," H interjects, remembering that M had lost his wife, Margaret, two years earlier. "Gathering bits and pieces remains the very stuff of legacy, doesn't it? So much rides on retrieving the nearly irretrievable. Speaking of memory, I remember my pleasure in seeing you, after decades, at the opening night of the exhibit Dialogue on the Gallop. I'd bet the photographs of galloping horses taken by Eadweard Muybridge, really central to the show that evening, were just a small part of Margaret's collection." Not being interrupted,

H continues, "Of course, I understand the connection—first, Margaret's passion for collecting photographs and, then, her dedication to writing and words. A formula for a thoughtful life: a passion for photography, writing and words. Or: for words, writing and photography. Yes? In any case, you have a big task ahead."

"Yeah, big," sighed M. "I'm going back through the photography we collected, inventorying, documenting it, deciding what to do with it: what to keep, what to offload. Vintage black and white, some color—not much color, mostly black and white. Margaret was both visually-oriented and literary—both sides of her brain activated—visually feeding off words and vice-versa. Her vision, I mean, is the collection. I learned a lot from her; she changed my way of seeing," M said. "And you, what are you up to? What are you writing?"

H always feels uneasy speaking about his writing; there is little he can comfortably share about how he spends his days. He knows that he is in a holding pattern, of sorts, writing about the people he is meeting, often on the street, creating a mosaic of characters, and, like M, piecing together memories, and, sometimes, taking photos, photographing the city in still shots, black and white. He might attempt to answer M's question with some of these words; H manages to get a few out, he thinks. "Walks I take; chance meetings on the street; black and white pictures; idle thoughts about books and time with friends, with a short novel eventually in mind." He means to stress the words: walks, friends, books and photographs, but he isn't certain; maybe he has only stammered, mostly incoherently.

At some point, M mercifully interrupts H with another question, "Do you know the work of W. G. Sebald? The *Rings of Saturn*... sounds a lot like Sebald..." M then turns to C, "doesn't it?"

C, who has apparently read much more Sebald than M, looks up from her arroz con leche—they are on dessert by now, "Yes," she agrees, "in his novel *Austerlitz*, mainly, and also in *The Rings of Saturn*, in the way he weaves images and words into the telling of a meandering story, moving through the East Anglia countryside. The use of grainy black and white photos, almost blurred, sometimes very narrowly focused—all around the notions of collective and individual memory, of loss, of changing perspectives of the past and present. What you're doing sounds not unlike the concepts Sebald was working with."

H always listens closely to what C has to say; he recalls what she wrote about his short story, "Transitions In Oaxaca." H feels that she is among the few who understood the story. And because he wants to remember to thank her, he has scribbled in his notebook some of her sentences: "You've caught perfectly," C had written, "the 'culti' Oaxaca scene of the galleries and the openings... where everyone knows everyone and everything...." But H most likes that *amber slumber* were C's favorite two words of his story; they are also his. He remembers that night back in the hotel after the exhibition the amber-colored-dream waves lasting long after the taste of mezcal reposado had dissipated. Stuck under his desk, he had wanted to write down more of the words that came to him in the dream, to make something of them. C had also written, "We [the readers] come back [days later] from the befuddled dream [H's] to the same art gallery but without any dialogue, or pretension, simply children [on a school outing]; a stark contrast to the 'cultured' opening night as they engage with the work in a far different way." Yes, H thinks again of what he saw at the gallery: the visiting school kids, drawing in a safe place, in the warmth of Oaxaca's midmorning, drawing their thick-black-pencil versions of Selma's ceramic work. These new meanings of "Transition" mean a lot to H. (H received other messages from friends about the stories in *Oaxaca and Beyond*; R and his companion K had missed the opening night at the gallery because of an unprovoked black wasp attack on R in his rock garden. R wrote to H: "... a gift to the Oaxaqueños." H hasn't seen R for months; nonetheless, they remain the dearest of friends; H has a few.)

At a nearby table, shaded by one of the restaurant's two patio trees, a couple speaks in tender tones to one another in Catalan, distracting H. And then, jarred back to the moment at hand, H realizes that C's reference to Sebald's writing, "weaving images and words into the telling of a meandering story," deserves some reaction on his part. H finally responds, "I have not read W. G. Sebald, but what you say about his experiment with prose and photography sounds intriguing; I'll read him soon... *The Rings of Saturn*—I like the title—for sure. Inhaling, still looking at C, H continues, "My time spent with West African mask sculptors, in Burkina Faso and Mali, stretched over a decade or two, influenced me the most... I mean in the use of photographs to move prose. But when I write, I also think of others, the writers whose books I still have on my bookshelves: Camus, Robbe-Grillet, and Duras—especially Camus, his spare prose and deliberate ambiguity, his recasting of older ideas of realism. I wonder if Sebald read these writers? — but, of course, he did," H quickly adds. Without mentioning any other names, H thought of the pleasure he takes in reading the stories, especially the short novels or short stories, of Ousmane Sembène, Raymond Carver, Juan Villoro, and Roberto Bolaño. But he has talked too much. By asking another question, maybe he can deflect the conversation away from himself: "There's tension in the air here in Oaxaca these days." H now turns to M. "What do you make of the anti-gentrification sentiment, the 'gringos fuera,' graffitied on building walls? Have we gringos overstayed our welcome in Mexico?"

"Well, H, I'm the first—or, maybe the second, behind you—to admit there are too many gringos here; their presence is what has brought this on." But, in his journalistic pursuit of facts, M continues, "I would guess that 60% of Oaxaca's tourism these days is Mexican and that 90% of the investment that drives gentrification—hotels, restaurants, bars, clubs, boutiques, tour operators, hostels—is Mexican from other parts of Mexico, some of it legit, some not. So, to equate gentrification solely with gringos is, at least in part, to scapegoat gringos."

At these last words, H notices that C is nudging M with her elbow: it's time to move on. While M speaks, H is trying to remember what exactly he said to M about the gringo issue. Many Americans have recently moved to Oaxaca, trying to make ends meet on a social security check. Maybe H said something acerbic about his fellow Americans, those who never seem to make much of an effort to learn Spanish and as a result remain apart from Oaxacan culture.

These three friends end the conversation with M mentioning the region of La Cañada, where J and A, photographer and social historian, travel frequently. "We've never been up there and are feeling a little stuck inside Oaxaca city, so we might go up for a few days. There's apparently a cave there with the oldest paintings known in Mesoamerica ... sounds really interesting. Would you like to go?"

H knew he would like to go. He didn't say so just then. Maybe Q, who would be arriving in a month or two, would like to join them.

There are other late afternoon meetings with M and C over delicious meals in the usual restaurants, El Pipe, El Cabuche or El Asador Vasco, the last two both in the center of Oaxaca. And then there are also long agreeable hours over tapas at El Olivo, or further out, away from the central area, over Istmeñan food at La Teca. But no matter the happenings of the day, H takes one last walk in the parks close by. On occasion, he sees E polishing the shoes of another client; or, more often, E has dozed off in his chair. Except for a few homeless people and young lovers kissing on dark, fretwork benches, the public squares and parks are deserted. E is always the last bootblack to leave the plaza, the last to wheel his mobile canvas stall (un puesto) to a nearby safe spot. H remembers E saying that it takes him about twenty minutes to get home at night on a bus.

Leaving the restaurant El Cabuche, H walks east on Calle Hidalgo to Avenida Juárez, where he turns left towards El Parque Llano. A stroller by nature, H stops to read the graffitied messages on the walls or to gaze at their art. He has long understood that Oaxaca de Juárez engages the flâneur in the issues of the day—graphically asserting that the city's streets and public spaces are not uniquely for the pleasure of the casual tourist.

Gringo Gentrificador

Gringo Gentrifier. "Is gentrification in Oaxaca really about too many gringos?" M had asked H. Graffiti on the walls pulse with current political and social issues. They are rarely effaced or painted over, even when they may not reflect a majority opinion. Time and rains eventually rub out most.

GRAFFITIED WALLS, URGENT MESSAGES

Viva Palestina Libre: Long Live Free Palestine

Could the urgent message above, Viva Palestina Libre, have been authored by someone from the many Indigenous pueblos who make up the rich diversity of the state of Oaxaca? Might distinctly different communities, separated by oceans, find common cause in a shared, violent colonial past? H can't answer these questions. Yet, he is certain that the "voices" of the walls of Oaxaca de Juárez offer up a public discourse—a narrative meant for Oaxaca and for a much larger community.

Compassion for the Palestinians is palpable these days in the city, as the Israeli Defense Forces exact their brutal revenge on the people of Gaza for the Hamas attack on Israel on October 7, 2023.

Las Fronteras Matan

Borders Kill. Sidetracked, daydreaming, H takes a detour up Calle Porfirio Díaz, heading without forethought in the direction of one of his favorite bookstores, El Ático. Just before reaching the store's front door, on a nearby building, he reads, "Las Fronteras Matan," "Borders Kill"—an admonition to the Oaxaqueños and others who cannot resist the siren call of the northern border. A flower's beauty appears as a treacherous tentacle of seduction luring desperate migrants to their deaths.

Mujer en el Blanco

Woman in the Bullseye. Street art in Oaxaca is often a call to action, a social engagement. H can't remember the location in Oaxaca where he stopped in awe of this mural: a women tethered by rattle snakes in front of a target's bullseye. At some point, he asks J for her reaction to this mural. J explains that the subject of the mural is "courage"—the courage with which this woman faces present-day violence.

Is the mural a vivid reminder of the sombra colectiva, the collective shadow, that challenges many countries, including the U. S. and today's Republic of Mexico? In his short story, "Transitions in Oaxaca," H quotes M's interview with S. In the interview S, the visual artist, makes clear the social and aesthetic underpinnings for her own art: she offers a visual text requiring a different "reading." S elaborates, "[I am] really investigating [in this present exhibition] memory and the collective shadow. Time becomes dysphasic.... The asymmetry of my work... an intuitive process... an endless series... like a loop, back and forth between the real object and its representation... open up possibilities for new readings... almost always starts from autobiographical... but very whimsical, as well... there is a response to anthropocentrism, to patriarchy."

Yes, S's art offers a context and a response to the condition of this courageous tethered woman, H thinks.

Ni una más

Not one more. H reads this as, Ni una mujer más: Not one more woman. But, of course, it could also be completed as, Ni una víctima más: Not one more victim; or perhaps as, Ni una violación más: Not one more rape.

It is the beginning of November, near the Zócalo, when H reads these charged words on a wall where Calle Valdivieso becomes Calle Macedonio Alcalá. J has reminded H that November 25th is the day that Mexico celebrates El Día contra la Violencia de Género — also known as El Día Internacional para la Eliminación de la Violencia contra las Mujeres. In the local newspapers, H has also read, El Día de Lucha contra la Violencía Feminicida.

El Futuro Es Nuestrix

The Future Is Ours. In Spanish, an assertive cry that could mean: Que está por venir, que todavía no es pero va a ser: What is to come, that is not yet, but will be. This mural is signed; however, H can't read the signature. When H shows the photograph to J, she calls it "La Canasta." "The Basket." H feels that J is taken by the mural's message. He wonders if she might write about it one day soon; he hopes so.

H looks again at the word NUESTRX. Would this be the future of authentic gender equality?

THE LEATHER MAN, EL FIBRACEL

Always, soon after his arrival in Oaxaca, H buys several new shirts and a new belt in his favorite clothing store, just off the Zócalo on Calle Hidalgo. Today, this Friday after his buys, he continues walking west on Calle Hidalgo, crossing south through the Zócalo. He cuts over a couple of streets to El Mercado Benito Juárez. Inside the enormous market, cheek by jowl, crowds of shoppers move in unpredictable waves down endless aisles. Close to one of the entrances, H finds F seated in front of his shop.

With a strong handshake and equally strong voices, H and F greet one another, "How are you Don F? How have you been these months? It's been awhile."

"Yes, we haven't talked for months. I'm feeling old, H, older and older. How's your writing going? Did your book come out? And the new book, stories about us Oxacans?"

And then, as if entering the western world's last trading post for the first time, H stares at all the merchandise that F, best known by his nickname El Fibracel, has managed to pack onto the multiple shelves; they display anything that anyone could want: miniature pearl chess sets, multicolored decks of playing cards, agricultural machetes, Masonic ceremonial swords (which could be only facsimiles), rows of small and large Swiss knives, and locks, padlocks of every size and shape, tools and tools for every job, and especially leather wallets and belts. "The leather is stamped 'Oaxaca,' but it's really from Chiapas and Jalisco; we Oaxacans can't get it together to produce our own leather," F says with measured derision.

Wait a minute, H says to himself, how many miniature fake pearl chess sets could F possibly sell? Really! And at that moment two young, tall German women appear in front of the stall and ask for a miniature chess set. Incredible coincidence, H muses, all the way from Berlin to buy a miniature chess set in Oaxaca.

Regaining his composure, after witnessing what must have been divine intervention with the sale of the chess set, H remembers another one of the reasons that brought him to the market today: it's to ask F to shorten a new belt. "F, I have this new belt, but it doesn't fit me properly. Can you please cut and size it for me, exactly the same way as before?"

Belts and belts ago, H had come in need of the same help. Walking among all the market stalls selling leather items, H had stopped in front of F's; H himself wasn't certain why he had chosen to approach F. Maybe there was a resolve, a fixed concentration in F's body, even noticeable when he was seated in his work chair, a man handsome in his time, still sturdy, one could say. Later, H is surprised to learn that F is in his late 80s.

Visits followed, sometimes weeks or months apart; long conversations had made a bridge to friendship. F had been retired for decades from his work in the mountains, the Sierra Juárez—lands of the Zapotec and the Mixtec peoples. There, F had measured felled timber (pine and Holm oak) for a lumber company that cut trees with permission from Zapotec and bordering Mixtec municipalities. The lumber company then reported F's measurements back to the Zapotec or Mixtec authorities.

"After leaving the encampment of eighty or more men in the mountains, I was by myself," F explained. "For years, I was the only one doing that kind of work. I didn't need to look for anyone to relieve the solitude of nature; I always had a book with me. Now I can overcome loneliness because I worked for fourteen years alone much of the time in the mountains of the Sierra Juárez." With characteristic calm, F then described his present life, "Those men, who worked with me in the mountains, come to see me here, and also those who competed with me in cycling come to visit me every month or so. But I can take care of myself; I don't mind living alone. My wife and I have been divorced for a long time. We're still friends, but we don't see one another much. My wife also has a stall in the market; she's a good salesperson; she does well."

Although F mentioned his wife, H didn't ask any questions about her, and only during other visits did he inquire more about cycling. Instead, he wanted to ask how F made ends meet. Did he sell enough to take care of his needs? "You've been retired a long time, and life in Oaxaca—well, life everywhere—has become more expensive." H wondered what response this obliquely asked question-statement might elicit.

"I'm okay; in a good month, I sell twice what the rent is for my stall in the market. And I get a small pension for my work in the mountains, and also a social security check from the federal government. It's enough for food, since social security pays for most of my medical bills. My days are pretty much the same; I always have breakfast—a cup of coffee with milk and a poached egg. For lunch, beans with cheese or chicken soup (caldo de pollo colorado). At least once a week I have fish, fried fish, mojarra (tilapia) for lunch. From the whole fish, I use the head and tail for broth soup. I don't have dinner. I read in the evening, always the same newspaper, El Imparcial, and I read and reread Cervantes and a few other books. I never watch television; I'm not interested in that culture. (While F talks, H takes some notes in his pocket notebook, and then shows or reads them to F for his approval.)

"We're both old men, Don F; in any case, sometimes I think of myself that way, as old. Do you think much about the past and perhaps have regrets?"

"Yes, I think sometimes about the past, but have few regrets. Well, maybe one, I was invited once, a long time ago, to become a Freemason; my wife objected, saying they were people of little faith. But, of course, she was wrong about that."

Much later, F told H that he'd been the long distance cycling champion of the state of Oaxaca for two consecutive years, "Fui campeón de Oaxaca, 80-160 kilómetros, 1956-1957, bicicleta de carreras, gracias al aire del monte." "I was champion of Oaxaca, 80-160 kilometers, 1956-1957, racing bikes, thanks to the mountain air." With subdued pride, F shared with H the meticulously saved newspaper (El Imparcial) clippings from those years. H read: "[Él] llegó al ciclismo de una manera circunstancial; pero lo vivió intensamente de tal suerte que en corto tiempo implantó récords, que después de 42 años aún permanecen imbatibles." "[He] came to cycling in a roundabout way, but he lived it intensely and with such luck that in a short time he established records that even after 42 years remain unbeatable." At the time, H wondered why the journalist had written the words, "roundabout way." But he forgot to ask.

On this late afternoon in January, F confided to H that he would continue to work and prepare for death at the same time: "Maybe I'll work one more year; that might be enough work, retire when I'm 87, that might be a time to die." He went further: "La muerte no me da miedo. Sé que la Biblia es ... muchos nombres que aprender. Prefiero hablar de Don Quixote, '... ladran los perros, Sancho, señal que cabalgamos.'"

"Death doesn't frighten me. I know the Bible is ... many names to learn. I prefer to talk about Don Quijote, '...the dogs are barking, Sancho, time to saddle up.'"

Not seeing the situation as quite so cut-and-dried, H replied, "Well, Don F, let's think this over ... the two of us together; instead of 'that might be a time to die,' let's say that we both agree we'll have fifty more lunches together... of course, we'll keep track." And H, grinning, stood up to leave, and headed down the aisle. Rounding the corner to the right, passing a silver jeweler's shop, H looked back and waved a last good-bye. F was laughing, both arms high, in a victory gesture.

H exited Mercado Benito Juárez at the main entrance on Calle Las Casas and walked into the late afternoon brume.

A Ceremonial Sword

F's shop in the Benito Juárez Market offers just about any item one might need. On this particular visit it's the Masonic ceremonial sword that catches H's eye. When F notices this, he tells H the story about the time the Freemasons invited him to join the Masonic lodge in Oaxaca: "I was invited to become a Freemason; my wife objected, saying they were people of little faith. But, of course, she was wrong about that." H admitted to F that he didn't know much about the history of Freemasonry in Mexico; he thought, however, he remembered the revered Oaxacan Benito Juárez had been a Freemason, as had other Mexican presidents and leaders. H wondered how many objects in F's store held untold stories. Long minutes often passed in silence between them. Maybe, they would have more time to talk about such things?

Cowhide Belts

Like other nearby shop venders, F has racks of cowhide belts for sale, some stitched with fancy woven cotton, some with western designs, others (not in the photo) more simple without embossing.

"Oaxaca must produce quite a bit of leather?" H asks.

46

F shoots back, "The leather is stamped 'Oaxaca,' but it's really from Chiapas or Jalisco; we Oaxacans can't get it together to produce our own leather," F adds with some derision.

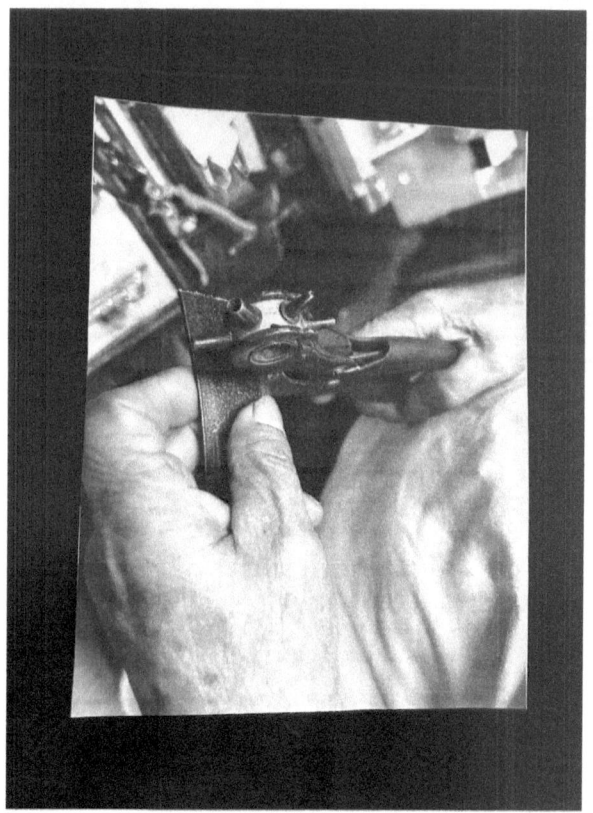

Leather Punch

H watches F cut his belt and then grip a leather punch in order to size the new belt just right. H would have enough belts to last through the decade. But, of course, that wasn't the point. It was about friendship in the moment.

Stillness.

H asks, "Is it lunch time, F? I always enjoy eating at La Abuelita, next door."

A Typical Diner

La Abuelita, a typical and popular diner in the 20 de Noviembre Mercado, is only steps away from F's shop. Although not his favorite eating spot in the market—F finds it a little expensive—on this afternoon, he agrees to eat here. They take bench seats. F orders an horchata drink, H a bottle of Ciel water, followed by a consomé con arroz, verduras y pollo for F, and mole negro con arroz y pechuga de pollo for H. They skip dessert. Later, F says his favorite diner is Comedor Catita in the same market. "There they prepare lunch and serve it the same day."

OF SNAKES & TERRORISTS

H leaves the Mercado Benito Juárez that Friday feeling some optimism in the presence of F's enduring energy. But now, once again in the street, he yields to the day's gray haze that dogs him.

A few days earlier, H had received a text message from his friend Ab, a Burkinabè guide and artist who knows more about the history of the masks of Burkina Faso than anyone H has met. Ab has seen H through thick and thin in West Africa on many occasions. In part, Ab's message reads:

"*Bonjour cher ami,*

J'espère que vous allez bien ainsi que toute la famille. Je vais bien. En famille c'est ma mère qui est souffrante. Elle a été mordue par un serpent à deux reprises dans la soirée du mardi. Où elle est, la ville est sous blocus terroriste. Il y a manque de sérum anti-venimeux dans les officines. Malgré tout, les infirmiers font de leur mieux en attendant l'arrivée du produit. Quant à mon village la situation n'est pas stable. Souvent c'est calme pendant un certain temps et soudainement il y a des attaques. La dernière attaque a eu lieu à la mine artisanale non loin du village. Comme c'est le début de la saison pluvieuse les terroristes multiplient les attaques partout pour que les gens ne puissent pas travailler dans les champs. C'est une stratégie, mais les gens ne fléchissent pas même au prix de leur vie.

Portez-vous bien. Je vous embrasse.

Amicalement,

Ab"

H immediately translates his messages from Africa because he wants to share them with C and M.

"*Hello, dear friend,*

I hope that you and your family are well. I'm all right. In the family it's my mother who is ill. She was bitten two times by a snake on Tuesday evening. The town is blockaded by terrorists where she lives. There's a shortage of antivenom serum. Despite everything, the nurses are doing their best while waiting for the serum to arrive. Here in my village the situation is not stable. Often, it's calm for a while, and then suddenly there are attacks. The last attack took place at the local mine not far from the village. As it is the beginning of the rainy season, the terrorists are doubling their attacks everywhere so that people will not be able to work the fields. This is [their] strategy, but people are not weakening even at the cost of their lives.

Take care of yourself. Hugs.

Yours ever,

Ab"

Earlier, before the bad news about his mother, Ab had described to H what life was now like in his village in Burkina Faso:

"Bonjour mon cher ami,

J'espère que vous allez bien ainsi que la famille. Comment se passe le séjour au Mexique? Mon village continue de s'effondrer par la force des terroristes. Dans la soirée les terroristes ont attaqué le village, pillé et incendié la mairie. Ils ont enlevé un infirmier dont on n'a pas de nouvelles. Le lendemain ils ont enlevé un homme de la famille qu'ils sont allés exécuter. Les enlèvements sont devenus leur monnaie courante. Les soirs aucun homme ne dort chez lui. Il y a ceux qui ont carrément quitté le village dont je fais parti.

Les réseaux téléphoniques sont coupés dans la commune suite au sabotage des infrastructures.

Les paysans ont du mal pour récolter. Dans certains endroits les terroristes interdisent les gens d'aller dans les champs.

Le Faso a subi un autre coup d'état .... Encore un militaire au commande de l'état, ce perpétuel coup de force conduira le pays dans le gouffre.

Je devais vous écrire bien avant, mais avec la succession des événements et le choc c'est maintenant que je commence à raisonner.
Portez-vous bien, surtout bon séjour au Mexique,
Je vous embrasse,
Ab"

"Hello, my dear friend,
I hope that you and your family are well. How is your stay in Mexico going? My village continues to collapse under the weight of the terrorists. In the night they attacked the village, pillaged, and set fire to the town council building. They kidnapped a nurse whose whereabouts remain unknown. The day after, they kidnapped a man whom they executed. Kidnappings have become commonplace. At night, no man sleeps at home. Some have simply left the village; that's my case.

The telephone networks have been cut in the district as a result of the sabotage of the infrastructure. Harvesting is difficult for the farmers. In certain places, the terrorists forbid the people to go to their fields.

The Faso [Burkina Faso] has suffered another coup d'état .... Another military man in command of the country, this never-ending show of force that will take the country to the depths of despair.

I should have written you much sooner, but with the succeeding events and shock, it's only now that I've begun to think clearly.

Take care of yourself, an especially good stay in Mexico,
Hugs, Ab"

A Green Snake, Ab's Mother

Ab sent these two photos: the first of the dead, long green snake (a Jameson's mamba, H conjectures—skin a dull green, measuring perhaps 6 feet); and a second of his mother's wounded, swollen foot. She was bitten while working just outside her home in a small garden plot.

This morning, Ab wrote again to H: *"Ma mère va beaucoup mieux aujourd'hui. Elle me charge de vous transmettre ses salutations."*
"My mother is much better today. She asks that I give you her greetings."

A few sentences followed, describing the scarcity of food and the increase of prices in this region of Burkina Faso:

"Dans la région ... les paysans peuvent seulement exploiter les champs les plus proches... Ces champs ne sont que des lopins de terre. Cela a engendré la crise alimentaire dans plusieurs endroits du Faso. Les prix des produits alimentaires ont inexorablement augmenté cette année dû à la baisse de la production agricole."

"In this area ... the farmers work only the closest fields... These fields are only patches of earth. This results in a food crisis in several locations of Burkina Faso. Food prices have inexorably risen this year due to the decrease in agricultural production."

Adding to the demoralizing news from Ab, H also has received somber emails from Mamadou, from the Dogon Country of Mali, which evoke vivid images of the havoc wreaked there by heavily armed men. As in Burkina Faso, terrorists, using similar brutal tactics, have made life unbearably fragile—especially for village farmers living at the foot of the Bandiagara Escarpment. This area includes the clay cliff dwellings of the Tellem, people who were there before and are no more.

Like Ab, Mamadou has remained in contact with H over the years, although it has been more than a decade since H last walked with him and visited with Mamadou's family in Mali. This is because, beginning in 2012, Mali is a country under almost constant siege: a country suffering from the scourge of perpetual violence, fanned by the practices of colonialism, religious extremism, old ethnic antagonisms, and different modes of existence—farmers versus nomads.

H answers Mamadou's anguished messages, even though he realizes he cannot assuage his friend's despair. In his emails, he asks after Mamadou's parents, onion farmers, cultivating fields high on the plateau of the Bandiagara. Mamadou and a blind Hogan, the spiritual leader in one of the villages of the Commune of Sangha on the Bandiagara, have often been resources for H, answering his questions about the old ways of the Dogon People.

Photojournalist Judith Romero and Wall-Size Poster of Tía Chona

J stands with her photograph next to the poster she hung. This photo is also the cover of the anthology, Oaxaca and Beyond. Thereafter, on his evening walks, H is drawn to this street La Calle Benito Juárez, corner Calle de Berriozábal—a street of dreams. He imagines the force that spoke to Aunt Chona when J readied her camera and Aunt Chona placed the cactus flowers over her own eyes. With this gesture, in this instant, was she taking back the photo to make it her own—or was this simply a playful act of creativity? Both, perhaps.

AUNT CHONA & THE COVER OF THE ANTHOLOGY

OAXACA & BEYOND: BILINGUAL MICRO FICTION FROM THE HEART

H hadn't seen much of J or A since the opening for the exhibition, Dialogue on the Gallop, at the Centro Fotográfico Manuel Álvarez Bravo. The show featured works by Selma Guisande, a Mexican visual artist, and the photographs of Eadweard Muybridge. H's short story, "Transitions in Oaxaca," recounted their meeting at the exhibit. In the intervening months, H has heard from other friends that A and J left Oaxaca to lecture at universities in Brazil and Argentina, and that this would take them away from Oaxaca for several months.

Now, back in Oaxaca, H is cheered by news about his short story, already published in the US. And the same anthology is about to come out in Oaxaca. But even after a long, brisk walk in the Parque Llano, he is unable to fall asleep. Although late November, the weather is still unusually warm, and, in consequence, the mosquitoes have never gone away. (These almost-microscopic nighttime pests leave indelible red glyphs on any exposed limb.) Finally, making the capital decision to give up on sleep, at least for awhile, H lathers his arms and hands with insect repellent, props himself up in bed with all the available pillows, and begins to reread a few lines from his own story, the words that A used to describe J and her photography and her documentaries on Afro-Mexican women:

59

"J has been exploring from a feminist perspective the decisions women make. I mean the decisions they're forced to make, living within their cultural constraints. Her photographs, ... Her interviews with indigenous women... Taboos... Those forced decisions that women confront."

That's it, H thought. Rereading these words about J's work settled it! The editors of *Oaxaca and Beyond* need to choose one of J's photos for the cover, the photo of an Afro-Mexican woman, titled "Tía Chona." He had seen the photo before in one of J's exhibits.

The next morning, H reads an article by A in which he describes J's latest work and her continued commitment to social justice. J's extended visits of documentation take place in the region of the Cañada, about seventy-five miles north of the city of Oaxaca in the small town of Valerio Trujano. According to A, J remains determined that her art, her images, will give back more than they carry away from an Afro-Mexican population that has been historically marginalized and whose heritage has often been appropriated by a consumer-driven culture.

The following week, H receives a text message from J, "Hello, H, I've heard that you're back in the city. That makes me happy. Can you come on a walking tour of the center of Oaxaca? Its subject will be the facades of buildings and their historical significance. Our tour begins this Saturday at 4pm in Avenida Juárez, corner Berriozábal, in front of the old cinema Ariel 2000. I'd really like you to come, H. I have a surprise for you."

Always punctual, H shows up at 4 in the afternoon at the spot described by J, just off the Parque Llano. Even forewarned by J, he is taken entirely by surprise by a huge poster of a photo plastered on the weathered door of the old cinema. From across the street, J motions and calls out to

H, "I told you!" And there, silhouetted by the chiaroscuro of still-glowing afternoon sun, was the photo of Aunt Chona. In complete self-possession, Aunt Chona fills, border-to-border, the photo that J took of her in the village of Valerio Trujano, the photo that H wanted for his book's cover.

During the walking tour of the crumbling, still beautiful, facades of Oaxaca, H asks J if she will tell him more about her visits to the Cañada region and the stories behind her photos from Valerio Trujano. They fix a day and time to meet in her studio, just in front of the well-known Instituto Blaise Pascale on Calle Dr. Gilberto Bolaños.

An Afternoon in J's Studio

Two days later, J greets H in the doorway of her studio with a warm embrace. "H, I'm glad to see you. I want you to see some of my work in Valerio Trujano. I know you have a special interest in Afro-Mexican communities; I remember when you shared your research in Africa and your African mask photos with A and me." Leading H by his elbow, J continues, "Come in, have a seat."

In a city known for its art, J's name is one of the most prominent among photographers and documentary photographers. Born in Vera Cruz and on her own since she was eighteen, she must have had some low times among her successes. H doesn't ask her about those times.

One by one, J shows H her photos of the town of Valerio Trujano and photocopies each for him. When back in his hotel the next morning, he reads and translates the photo captions written by J; maybe A's pen is also present. H edits and adds to some of the captions, keeping all in the pine drawer of his bedroom desk. He will go back to these photos and captions in the days to follow, adding notes to himself, retrieving, the conversation he had with J.

J and a Panoramic View of the Region of the Cañada, Oaxaca

J's caption beneath this photo: "The region of the Cañada has not been studied much, especially regarding the Afro-Mexican populations that live there. The Cañada has a great biodiversity, as found in its surprising desert landscapes that make it strangely unique and creative, as are the black communities who inhabit, close to the ocean, the coast. El Rio Grande—running through and connecting regions and channeling into the river called Papaloapan—is considered important for the economic, social and recreational life of the community; furthermore, the hill in the background, known as Colorado, is both a visual and cultural reference for Cuicatlán's countryside."

H translated J's caption into English, in the evening, when he wasn't always at his best. H copied J's original caption in his notebook, so that he could get back to it, with a little luck, when he remembered:

"Vista panorámica de la región de la Cañada en la comunidad de Valerio Trujano, Oaxaca. La región de la Cañada ha sido poco estudiada, sobre todo en lo que se refiere a las poblaciones afromexicanas que la habitan. Posee una gran biodiversidad, así como sorprendentes paisajes de desierto, los cuales la hacen peculiar y distinta con el imaginario dominante sobre los pueblos negros a quienes los ubican cercanos del mar, habitando las costas. El Rio Grande—que interconecta regiones y deriva en el llamado rio Papaloapan—es considerado importante para la vida económica, social y recreativa de la comunidad; además, el cerro conocido popularmente como Colorado, es a la vez un referente visual y cultural del paisaje de Cuicatlán."

Entrance to the Town of Valerio Trujano, State of Oaxaca

During H's visit to J's studio, she described her earlier stays in the municipality of Valerio Trujano and her attention to the history of its people. In her photo documentary *Afrovalerianos: Memoria, territorio y alteridad*—a photo exhibition that has toured numerous Latin American countries—J stresses this history. About the photograph above, J explained, "I wanted the photo of a black Mexican woman of Valerio Trujano and of an important town wall to capture," J's voice grew even stronger as she finished the sentence, "a very significant date for this community. At at the same time, I wanted it to reflect my own real interest in the town's social history."

"Could you explain a bit more?" H interjected. "Could you say more about the principles guiding your work as a photographer and researcher? From my time in Africa and friendships sustained there, especially in villages in Burkina

Faso and Mali, I have a feeling for the care you take, care to integrate your photographs with a community's history, its individual people. Is 'care' the right word? What word would you use?"

"Yes," J continued speaking while leaving her worktable and drawing a metal stool closer to H. "I understand your question and what you're asking me. My documentary and visual work in Valerio Trujano was undertaken with patience. It was sustained through trust and collaboration that I built in the community; this is a long process, neither easy nor immediate, transpiring in conversations over months with those in charge and with the town's people. Only months of coexistence can form these bonds of trust. I'll leave it to you, H, to think about the words that reflect this process."

Back in his hotel, H had more time to think about the history to which J referred when they were both in her studio. H knew that slavery was outlawed in all of Mexico much before it had been in the United States with the 13th Amendment in 1865. Hunched over his desk, eyes fixed on the photo, H tried to fathom the courage of the people of Valerio Trujano. He imagined their firm resolve when they won their freedom in 1812. Could something of this firmness be seen in their faces now more than two hundred years later?

The Home of Uncle Odilón, Valerio Trujano

"First, H," J explains, "I was attracted by the welcoming smile of the boy, then by the fact this was a typical home of Valerio Trujano, one of the oldest, I thought. But the blue shirt caught my attention, and I stopped to ask if I could take a photo. No one changed in any way when I took the photograph; that was important to me." J continues, telling H that dwellings in Valerio Trujano are known as "the home of aunt or uncle so-and-so." And in town, "people refer to one another as uncle or aunt, or cousin, without being blood relatives. These are simply meant to be friendly words of respect." Later, J learns the name of the boy, Edwin Leyva Aguirre, who is with his uncle, Odilón Aguirre Alcalá. Odilón "at one time had an important position in the town and also knew many of its stories."

Afrovalerian Family, Valerio Trujano, Oaxaca

Among the people of her community, the Afro-Mexican woman, Señora Enriqueta Concepción Urrutia Astilleros, 86 years old, is known as Aunt Chona. She has worked all her life at various jobs, with her family in mind. In a conversation with J, she mentioned that the elders in her family did not have a portrait to pass on in remembrance of them to future generations. J wrote: "En una charla comentó la tía Chona que no tenían un retrato de familia que quedara como memoria para sus descendientes."

When J asked Aunt Chona where she would like to have the photo taken with her daughters—María Tecla and Elvira Hernández Urrutia, Maricruz and Lidia Alcalá Urrutia—she chose her adobe home, for all the life and memories that it held. At the agreed hour, as afternoon fell, everyone arrived, "dressed for the occasion." One had the impression that this family portrait had become an event—a kind of ceremony, memorable and unique.

J then wrote: "En la hora pactada, al atardecer, todas llegaron 'vestdas para la ocasión'. Daba la sensación de que el retrato fotográfico se convertía en un acontecimiento, como algo ceremonial, memorable e irrepetible."

J made it clear—more than once to H—that her photographs were not meant simply to capture a family moment. The photo above would not have an independent history. H understood that J's project was not undertaken to be solely about the production of images, but were instead grounded in a people's history—acknowledging, without artifice, both the people in front of and behind the camera. This was why H was drawn to J's work in La Cañada, undertaken in collaboration with A.

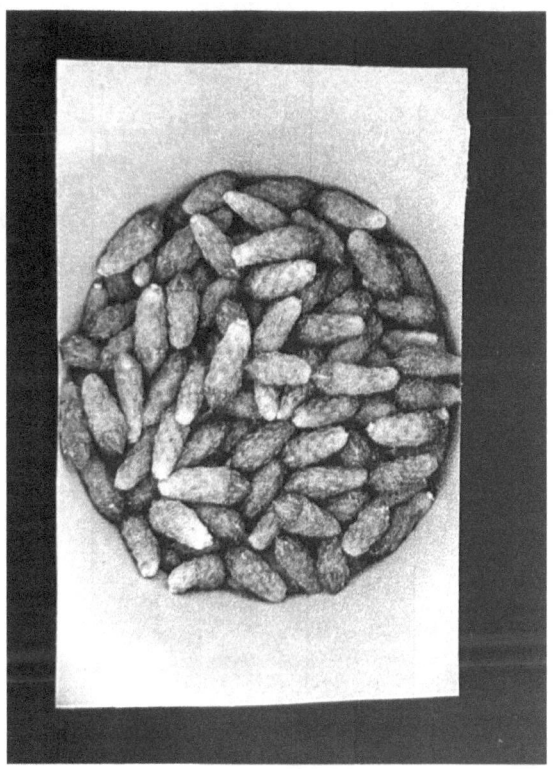

Little Cocochas, Valerio Trujano, Oaxaca

Aunt Chona rises at 6am to cut the cocochas, when it's early. She's been teaching her family, little by little, how to do this; she tries to start at sunrise, since the sun's heat can be intense from 10am on. The cococha, a kind of prickly pear cactus with sharp thorns, is best cut when there is little wind and sun. It is used for the mole of cococha, made during Lent, which Aunt Chona prepares every year as part of the traditional knowledge of this Afro-Mexican community. The cococha bud flowers with singular beauty, but once open it cannot be used in the mole.

THE RETURN TO
VALERIO TRUJANO

J returns to Valerio Trujano with photographs: "I understand the importance of returning often to Valerio Trujano," J tells H. "And to give back something to the community that, at first, might appear to be something that I took away."

STREETS & PARKS OF OAXACA

There are many reasons to come to Oaxaca. This time, H has come because he wants to be here for the Mexican publication of *Oaxaca and Beyond*. But, for H, there are other compelling reasons to be in Oaxaca: there's walking; he's always found solace in walking—peace in parks and mountains. The city also offers up vital, public spaces: its murals are painted voices, stories of myths and messages of social urgency, of deep class antagonisms, and of conflicts in human values. H doesn't usually walk farther than the center of Oaxaca, although he might walk as far north as the Colonia of San Felipe del Agua; to the south, he often walks briskly to the Mercado 20 de Noviembre—and maybe as far as the Central de Abastos, to the southwest of the Zócalo.

Traffic in certain parts of the city is intense, starting in late October until mid-Janauary. El Parque Llano and El Jardín Conzatti, both near H's hotel, offer retreats from the parades, music and ricocheting city noises.

On H's evening walk, the statue of Benito Juárez, moonlit in the center of the Parque Llano, appears more lifelike than usual. A man of humble Zapotec roots, famous for his respect for the rights of others, Benito Juárez served as president of the Republic of Mexico during the same period that President Abraham Lincoln resided in the White House. Historians have often imagined the conversation that the two famous jurists might have had, if they had truly met in person. H remembers that this meeting didn't happen. Today, both men—one six feet four inches tall, the other four feet six inches—share equally the lofty heights that history reserves for the few. H returns to gaze at this statue on many evenings. On this night, a cooling breeze sweeps over green cantera stones beneath the statue.

Benito Pablo Juárez García

An evening photo of the Oaxacan jurist and past president of the Republic of Mexico: at this hour, Benito Juárez doesn't have to worry about a strong sun in his eyes. A popular story that F once told H maintains that a governor of the state of Oaxaca was so concerned with this issue that he had the statue turned to face a setting, rather than a rising sun.

Tourism: Two Oaxacas

Above, one of the ubiquitous tour buses of Oaxaca, equipped with a blaring loud speaker, guides visitors through the center of the city. With its local color of an Indigenous dress of the Isthmus of Tehuantepec region of Oaxaca painted on the rear, a London-style bus passes by the capital's green spaces, colonial-era architecture, and many museums—ostensibly accessible to all. Yet, the city's emphasis on tourism is itself a reminder of the chasm separating the city center from daily life on the outskirts, la vida periférica. During another of H's stays in Oaxaca, Antonio Pacheco Zárate's novel, *Centraleros*, was published and became very quickly a best seller (un succès de scandale). Its notoriety and success, both well deserved, gave voice to the other Oaxaca—to those living a gritty life on the city's periphery; the novel's street-smart, sexually-free language, H muses, is probably not a vocabulary taught in the city's many Spanish language schools for international students.

MYTHS AND POWERS: The Muralists Jesús Kobe, Uriel Fernando Barragán, & a Rare Find

The walk from Calle Ignacio Allende and up Calle Panorámica del Fortín is more strenuous than other city walks. But after a lunch of black mazatecan mole, H is happy for the exercise. Not far into his walk, he engages for the second time with Jesús Kobe, a muralist. The first time, H had talked with Jesús Kobe in Calle Pino Suárez; H now knows that Kobe is a well-known Oaxacan artist, whose murals are in Spain, Germany, Holland, Israel and in many western cities in the US—San Francisco and Davis, California, as well as Portland, Oregon, and Prescott and Flagstaff, Arizona. Both men stop to talk further, in the shade of a nearby wall.

"I met you in front of the huge mural on Pino Suárez that you painted for the union representing Oaxacan physical education teachers. After that I looked at your website and saw a lot more of your art. It's a pleasure to see you again. I wonder if working on the street as you do, you're often interrupted?" At this point, H is smiling, somewhat sheepishly, but continues on, "Well, I interrupted you, myself, right in the middle of a video interview being conducted then on the street, on Pino Suárez. You stopped everything to say hello to me. Was it annoying?"

"No, not at all. Most of the time, I'm alone with my art; I paint and think, and I touch the walls of the buildings. But I also know that my art is public; it isn't studio art, and it isn't contained within the four corners of a building. I hope it has an immediate contact with people. As a muralist, I have the same connection with passersby; that's my intention."

Jesús then spoke of the role of the artist, "El artista es líder de opinión para preparar nuevas visiones, como Goya y William Blake." "The artist is an opinion leader in the preparation of new visions, like Goya and William Blake." Jesús also expressed a debt of gratitude to The Graphic Arts Institute of Oaxaca (El IAGO, El Instituto de Artes Gráficas de Oaxaca), more specifically to the school's founder, the artist Francisco Toledo. There was a hint of emotion in his voice when he said the name, Francisco Toledo.

This was the last time that H saw Jesús. Although they had wanted to meet up again, it never happened.

In parting, H's last words to Jesús were, "Poco a poco, entiendo lo que ofrecen las calles de Oaxaca."

"Little by little, I'm understanding what the streets of Oaxaca offer."

The Mural of Jesús Kobe on Calle Pino Suárez

On Calle Pino Suárez, across from Parque Llano, Jesús Kobe painted a huge mural for the union representing physical education teachers of Oaxaca. On one side, he depicts the classical world of western mythology, and on the other, the mythology of Mesoamerica. Are these two worlds in opposition to one another? Is their side-by-side positioning meant to underscore two equally powerful but different ways of giving meaning to life? With the depiction of the Mixtec divinity Dzahui, symbol of rain and patroness of the Mixtec nation, this mural of Mesoamerican inspiration emphasizes an eternal oneness with nature: water, humankind and community are inseparable in the ordering of the world.

Jesús told H that he received twenty-five thousand Mexican pesos (about $1,500, US dollars in 2024) in payment for this mural; he had bargained for two years with the union for this price.

A Detail of the Jesús Kobe Mural

This detail from the mural on Calle Pino Suárez shows a Mixtecan ball player with heavy, leather glove on his right hand; these gloves weigh from three to six kilos, or approximately seven to thirteen pounds. On the left side of the photograph, Kobe paints una porta de gol o anillo. These goals or rings were found on walls of the playing field, as seen today in the zone of Monte Albán, a part of the extensive Zapotec lands. On the right is a "macuahuitl,"— the broad, hardwood sword with razor sharp obsidian inserts, famously wielded by Aztec warriors during the Spanish conquest of Mexico.

As H has understood, the ballgame played here, El Juego de Pelota, is more properly described as a ritual with cosmic implications, i.e., a metaphor for life in Mesoamerica. In fact, the game appears to have been played from northern South America to the present-day states of Arizona and New Mexico. On this subject, H thinks it improbable that either the victors or the losers were sacrificed at the end of the game, as some historians have conjectured.

A Oaxacan from the town of Santo Domingo Tonalá in the region of Mixteca Baja, once told H that he played a version of the game when he visited his family in Napa, California; his family, uncle and cousins, work in the vineyards there. When H expressed a special interest in the glove worn during the game by Mixtecan players, his friend promised to bring back a glove for him, when he next visited Santo Domingo Tonalá.

An Indigenous Plumed Warrior With Crystalline Blue Water Flowing From His Cupped Hands

The second time H talked to Jesús Kobe, the artist was putting the finishing touches on this mural on Calle Panorámica del Fortín. As H was about to leave Jesús, a smiling woman suddenly stepped from the doorway next to the mural. She was, as it turned out, the owner of the home and the person who had commissioned the mural. Taking a step toward H, she explained that she had asked that the mural focus on the current scarcity of water and draw attention to the high prices that she and her neighbors were all being charged for its delivery.

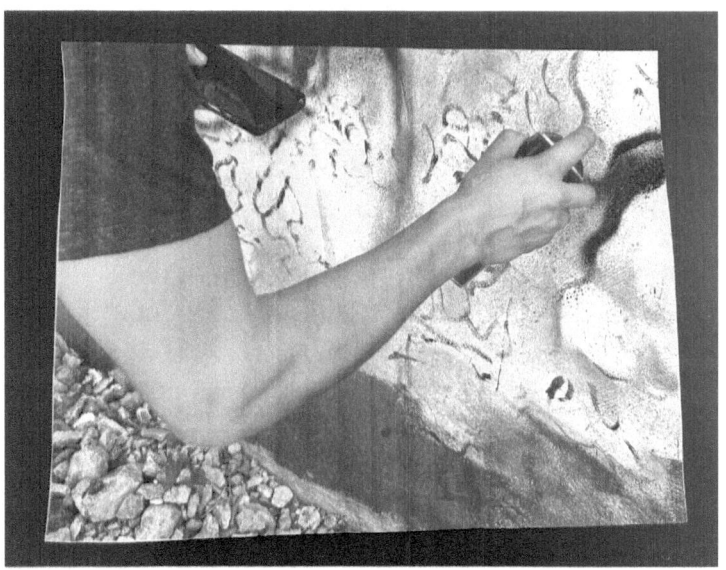

The Arm of the Muralist, Calle Panorámica del Fortín

Jesús, a tall muscular man, paints while H watches. "You probably wonder how I broke my nose. Well, I fell and broke my nose running from the police. I was eighteen. I'd been painting walls since the age of fourteen. I tripped and broke it in the street. The police were tough those years, that was part of life."

La Calle Panorámica del Fortín

A good walking street, Calle Panorámica del Fortín has small cafés, bakeries, delis and some of the largest and most dramatic murals in the city. H likes to start his occasional evening walk at Templo de Santo Domingo de Guzmán, on the Calle Constitución side of the church; there, at the southern entrance, on the wide cantera stones, young couples kiss tenderly in confident anonymity, and in the immediate foreground, an amplified jazz saxophonist plays with all the self-assurance of a young John Coltrane.

H finds the interior of the Templo disquieting with its gilded baroque exuberance. Thus, he rarely enters the church, preferring instead to linger, watch and listen to the crowds milling about on the church square. Even so, H often glimpses—through the open church doors—the frequent wedding parties, brides, grooms and their entourages in the chiaroscuro of the narthex, the west end of the church.

From the Templo de Santo Domingo de Guzmán, H walks west on Calle Ignacio Allende, and then bearing slightly to his left, engages Calle Panorámica del Fortín. While climbing the steep, narrow sidewalk with the street in a state of perpetual excavation and repavement, H wonders how life would be here, how it would feel to live in this middle class neighborhood, with cool air, hospitable people, and red and white geranium-laden patios.

The Muralist Uriel Fernando Barragán Cruz

In late afternoon, under a broken blue sky and ever-present cumulus clouds, H passes and then returns to a group of men deeply engrossed in conversation on Calle Pino Suárez; one among the group points emphatically across the street to the above mural. H soon finds out that this fellow is the artist, the Oaxaqueño, Uriel Fernando Barragán Cruz (AKA Bouler

Oaxaca). With the unfaltering good manners still much a part of the city, the muralist turns to welcome H, "Yes, my friend, this is a mural of the sacred dog, Xóloitzcuintle — the ancient Aztec dog — the dog that helps the dead, los fallecidos, cross the river on their way to Mictlán. Do you know Mictlán?" Answering his own question, Bouler continues, "It's the place of the dead."

In unpunctuated sentences, the muralist, sensing H's earnestness, offers further description of the myth of the dog, El Xolo. He explains that it's a myth stressing the importance of treating all animals here on earth with gentleness and respect. While the muralist speaks, H studies the mural; the dog is neither all black nor all white, but rather a shade of gray. H recognizes other symbols, the skull and the marigolds— all part of the commemoration of El Día de Muertos taking place these days; his favorite figure in the mural is the hummingbird, el colibrí. The hummingbird's energy and association with nectar and nourishment would surely be of great value for any trip through the underworld, the world of spirits, un viaje al inframundo, al mundo de los espíritus.

A Rare find

In the following days, H seeks out more Bouler murals; he sees several on the walls of the Jalatlaco barrio of the city. Jalatlaco, once a Zapotec village, is now a neighborhood favored by expats, an area of residential homes, art galleries and two bookstores, Amate and El Burrito Librería. With the Bouler murals in mind, H returns several times that same week to El Jalatlaco. On one fortuitous afternoon, H finds a used coffee table book that he has been looking for, *AFRO áfrica-cuba-méxico*, in El Burrito Librería. He knows that it has chapters by his friends, R and A.

Heavy book in hand, H accepts the invitation by the bookstore's owner to take a seat at a small, round table, just past the threshold. H is soon lost in his reading. At some point, though, he asks the price of the book. "It's on sale for 1000 pesos, about $60," the owner says. "It's a book that's no longer available these days. You don't really have to buy it. Don't feel obliged to. You may continue looking at it here."

While reading, for maybe an hour, H has copied passages in his notebook from the chapters written by R and A:

From René Bustamante's chapter: "A pesar... del evidente componente multiétnico de nuestro país y de su aparente aceptación en la sociedad mexicana, prevalece por un lado una gran desinformación y por otro una cierta tendencia a romantizar el grado de componente sanguíneo que cada uno tiene en sus venas de los descendientes de los esclavos africanos." R wrote this in his chapter, *"De África a Oaxaca Travesías de la cultura negra."*

"In spite of... the evident multiethnic makeup of our country and its apparent acceptance in the Mexican society, there prevails on one hand a grand disinformation, and on the other a tendency to romanticize the blood relationship that we have in our veins from the descendants of African slaves." From the chapter, *"From Africa to Oaxaca Dangerous Crossings of Black Culture."*

And from Abraham Nahon's chapter, *"La rebeldía solar de la negritud,"* ("The Solar Rebellion of Negritude"), H had hurriedly written down A's critical assessment of the place of the Afro-Mexican communities in a Mexico largely defining itself as a mestizo culture:

"La historia de América y de México sigue dominada por la visión eurocéntrica, desde la biología hasta la teología. Los negros o esclavos son considerados intrusos de nuestra historia .... Afromexicanos, afrodescendientes, afromestizos, afrolatinos, morenos o autoadscritos como negros (como sucede en la Costa Chica de Oaxaca), estas poblaciones subsisten actualmente sobre todo en Oaxaca, Guerrero y Veracruz, manteniendo una cultura viva y diferenciada...."

"The history of America and of Mexico continues to be dominated by a Eurocentric vision, from biology to theology. Blacks or slaves are considered intruders in our history .... Afro-Mexicans, Afro-descendants, Afro-mestizos, Afro-Latinos, dark-skinned or self-identified blacks (as found on the Costa Chica of Oaxaca) — these populations are present today in Mexico, above all in the states of Oaxaca, Guerrero and Veracruz, and are preserving a vital and distinctive culture..."

CUICATLÁN, VALERIO TRUJANO & THE CAVE OF SMALL HANDS

Nearing the end of H's stay in Oaxaca, M reminds him of the invitation to travel together to the town of Cuicatlán, a three-hour drive from Oaxaca city. From there, they could see the nearby ancient cave, La Cueva de Las Manitas. And since Cuicatlán is also close to Valerio Trujano, where J continues to spend time documenting the history of the community, they could also plan to walk in this small town.

H had not forgotten about the tentative trip with M, C and Q. And Q has just arrived from the States. She also likes the idea. So, M and H soon begin meeting for morning coffee in Café SL28 on Calle Reforma to plan the details — maps, car rental, hotel reservation, market visits in Cuicatlán, walks in the region, and local guides for the cave. (Q is attending Spanish language classes at Instituto Cultural Oaxaca in the mornings, and C is still working with a local program that provides food and clothing to migrants from the south.).

At first, they all agree to extend the road trip from Cuicatlán to the town of Huautla de Jiménez, in Mazatecan lands, another three hours away on Highway 182, in the northern part of the Cañada region. But as the trip draws nearer and time together shorter, all four think that they should stay in Cuicatlán, in the hotel recommended by A, and not go ahead to Huautla de Jiménez, after all.

Walls of History in Valerio Trujano

The morning after their arrival in Cuicatlán—and after a good night's sleep and breakfast at La Abuelita—Q, H, C and M drive twenty-minutes, passing through miles of dry, stoic forests of columnar cacti, to Valerio Trujano.

Close to the entrance of the town, on school walls—once a part of a sugar hacienda—murals greet all visitors. Their words proudly commemorate the community's heritage and history of freedom: TWO HUNDRED AND ELEVENTH ANNIVERSARY OF THE ABOLITION OF SLAVERY. Even J's photo documentation did not completely prepare them for the impact of this visual history, experienced in person. H takes photos along the same walls where J stood with her camera

As a polite gesture, M and C suggest that they make their presence known to the town's municipal president by introducing themselves.

A few steps away, in the the town's plaza, with the confidence of someone who, with her sister, had travelled for months in Mexico, writing about the country's highways and byways, C approaches a well-dressed older woman, asking her for the president's home address.

"The president is away today—don't worry—you're welcome here," the Valeriana says and moves on.

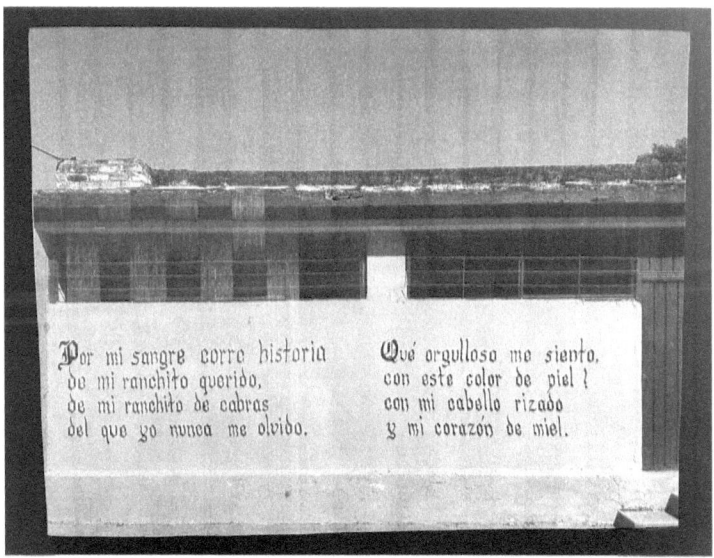

Another School Wall in Valerio Trujano—Bearing History's Weight

Through my blood runs history   How proud I feel,
From my beloved farm,   With this color of skin!
From my farm of goats   With my curly hair
That I never forget.   And my heart of honey.

These words, translated by H in his notebook, attach a people to Oaxaca's earth, words at odds with any "tendency to romanticize" the presence of Afro-Mexicans by today's larger Mexican society. These Valerianos are not "intruders," because of skin and hair.

Colonel Valerio Trujano, Center of Town, Valerio Trujano, Oaxaca

Seated alone in the quiet square of Valerio Trujano, H copies in English the Spanish words below the bust of the town's namesake: Colonel Valerio Trujano (1767 – 1812) "HERO OF THE 111 DAYS" FIRST INSURGENT FROM TEPECOACUILCO, GUERRERO

LIBERATOR OF THIS PUEBLO
IN MARCH 1812

The Colonel Valerio Trujano, himself a descendant of the first Africans brought to Mexico, becomes a hero for holding out 111 days in the siege of Huajuapan (in the actual State of Oaxaca) against the Spanish crown's royalist forces: in March 1812, Mexico was still a part of New Spain on the American continent. This historical event takes place during Mexico's long struggle for independence, September 16, 1810 to September 27, 1821.

Would their liberation in 1812 in Valerio Trujano have given former Black slaves an equal social and economic status in their community? H wonders how the Indigenous people and the mestizos of the town saw the new freedom of their Black fellow Valerianos?

Las Raíces de Mi Tierra

The Roots of My Land: A scene—a Hollywood-worthy freeze frame—that may never have existed. A mural in Valerio Trujano paints a Black woman who carries a perfectly balanced light jar.

Where are the roots of the Afro-Mexicans of this town? Historians often mention the present-day sub-Saharan countries of Cameroon, Angola, and the Democratic Republic of Congo as possible African points of departure to New Spain: these countries represent a vast area of Africa where Bantu languages are spoken—a linguistic family which includes hundreds of recognized languages, only sometimes mutually intelligible. H wonders if refinements in DNA studies and in linguistic science are now able to place geographically the multiple waves of Africans that arrived in Mexico.

Afro-Mexicans Harvesting Sugarcane and Picking Cactus

In the fields of Oaxaca, Black labor replaced that of the Indigenous peoples, whose ranks had long been decimated by disease and exhaustion. Oaxacan journalists have written that Black workers were brought to Valerio Trujano in 1861 by the local owners of the sugar factory. Were some of these freed Black workers already living in or near the town of Valerio Trujano? H is not sure.

Although idealized beyond credibility, might this mural open the door to a discussion of the history of the Afro-descendants of this town and of the surrounding region of La Cañada? H wonders what stories arise from the hearts of the people of Valerio Trujano. Are Black grandmothers and great grandmothers of Valerio Trujano retelling today the stories of their families to their children? Their stories would surely contrast with the idyll that this mural presents, H thinks.

The Aqueduct of Valerio Trujano

This remarkable structure still brings water to the town from the surrounding mountains kilometers away. Once its water powered the millstone that crushed and ground the sugarcane stalks in the hacienda's factory

The Church of Valerio Trujano, Iconography

At one point, Q, C and M visit the town's church. Q takes a photo of the altar's Black Christ. In the meantime, H goes to buy a bottle of cold water and to speak with the owner of the small grocery store, La Tia China.

As his friends come out of the church, H, walking towards them, can see they are animated in conversation, impressed by what they just saw. Although close, H can't make out what they are saying. And later, he and Q never return to the subject.

The Cave of Small Hands, the Footpath

Early, the final morning of their trip together, Q, H, C and M pack, check out of their hotel, and leave Cuicatlán. After breakfast, they meet up with their guides in the village of Santiago Dominguillo. Thanks to the Office of Tourism in Cuicatlán, they had contacted these guides days before and had agreed on the details of the visit to the cave.

"We are going to be fifteen minutes late," someone points out from the backseat of their rented Nissan. H isn't sure who says this.

Yes, H knows that they lingered too long over the breakfast table at La Abuelita in the outskirts of Cuicatlán. But there was singular good cheer when they were all together over meals. Among other dishes on the menu, they ordered empanadas de amarillo, followed by fresh mango—and several cups of black coffee, and then created together a replay of the soccer game they had watched the night before: fifteen-year olds, five on a team, all incredible artist-athletes, playing on a cement basketball court, a sort of elevated stage, just twenty feet away from where Q, H, C and M sat and ate still-steaming corn on the cob, slathered with mayonnaise, flakes of white cheese and chile and sparkling with fresh lime juice. "I'd like another one, H," Q had said, while tightening her grip on the stick of her elote.

"By the way, H, did you notice the title of the book I was skimming in the Office of Tourism the evening we were there?"

"Yes, I did ... glimpsed part of the title, Cuicatec Riddles And .... What did you get from it?"

"Well, the book—the full title caught my eye, *Cuicatec Riddles And Tone Twisters*, by Maestra Lucia Lezema Tejada. Tone Twisters! That made me realize Cuicateco is a tonal language. This teacher wants to spread the use of Cuicateco by teaching it in the classrooms. Wouldn't you like to know more? The book is trilingual—Spanish, Cuicateco, English. I'll try to find it online."

Now, finally, they leave the breakfast table at La Abuelita. After about a thirty-minute ride back on highway 135, they arrive at Santiago Dominguillo. On the outskirts of the village, their guides, Jenny, her fifteen-year-old daughter, Romi, and Jenny's companion, José, greet them.

From there, they travel on two ATVs in the direction of the cave, several kilometers away. The group's first stop is at a well-built mountain fence, where, after Jenny unlocks the gate's heavy padlock, they dismount and continue on foot. The rough, ascending foot path, bordered by razor-sharp spines of barrel cacti, demands constant attention—falling on these spines would mean sudden, excruciating pain, H judges. Before reaching the cave's entrance, they climb down several hand-hewn wooden ladders, side rails anchored to rock ledges.

A Home with a View, a Sacred Place

La Cueva de Las Manitas faces to the east in the region of the Biosphere of Tehuacán-Cuicatlán, a Unesco World Heritage Site since 2018. This protected world treasure covers close to 2,000 square miles, about 500,000 hectares, or 1,235,000 acres.

Looking out from the extraordinarily long and wide mouth of the cave, Q, H, C and M contemplate the vast wilderness of majestic mountain ranges: the ever present spiny shrubs, forests of pine-oak, and giant columnar cacti. The view from the sheer edge of the outcrop underscores the power of emptiness, of uninhabited lands under the sway of nature. Yet, people were here once, 12,000 years ago, hunting and gathering in this region of the state of Oaxaca. Does the cave's disproportionately large entrance suggest that its inhabitants felt some degree of security? Might they have hunted, fished, and gathered over undisputed, borderless mountains? More questions, unanswered by H.

Did these Indigenous Peoples — whose hundreds of hands bring life to the cave walls — pass on the languages overheard on market days in the town of Cuicatlán and in villages of the Valley of Tehuacán-Cuicatlán? Do the peoples (Cuicatecos, Mazatecos, Mixtecos, Popolocas, Chinantecos, Ixcatecos, and Nahua) carry today histories of ancient languages and archaic genes from a time when nature was a place of rich sounds and scents? Dramatic language and blood changes must have taken place when the descendants of the artists of this cave moved to the lower valleys, when their numbers grew larger with the advent of agriculture. What accumulated knowledge did they share in the valleys? What was lost?

When H and Q walk in the market of San Juan Bautista Cuicatlán, they know that they are listening to Indigenous languages. Sellers in the market's permanent stalls (puestos fijos) confirm this. And, as elsewhere in Oaxaca, on many occasions, there is the sharing of something personal, vital to the person telling the story: H and Q listen to a lady who occupies one of these stalls. Smiling and speaking in Spanish over the din of market day, she describes her ten difficult years as a cook in a Mexican restaurant in the US, in one of the Carolinas: "The restaurant owner kept us working many unpaid hours in the kitchen. We had no choice but to accept ... afraid to complain. I worked hard but saved truly little. Back in Oaxaca, in Cuicatlán, where I was born, I have my family and friends. I'm happy."

Inside and outside the market building, vendedores, sellers, are mostly women. Outside, H and Q listen to people selling, buying, and bargaining in Cuicateco. Sometimes, a seller, using Spanish, sells a whole vegetable plant por pieza, by the piece; sometimes, a buyer asks for una cucharada de, a tablespoon of; un medio kilo de, a half kilo of; un medio litro de, a half liter of; una bolsita de, a small bag of. Sounds and scents of measuring and buying meld in the humid air. Bananas, corn, squash, limes, mangos, eggplants, quelites ... and many other foods whose names H forgets to write down and can no longer remember. During the rains a variety of mushrooms are available in the market. There are also stands offering medicinal herbs, traditional medicines, requiring patience and guidance to know how to use.

Rock Paintings in the Cave of the Small Hands

Pinturas rupestres, cave paintings — red, ocher, white, and black, remarkably vivid — reach all the way to the entrance of La Cueva de Las Manitas. In modern times, in the 1970s, Rafael Cruz Vázquez found the cave. Jenny tells us that archeologists, on several brief visits from Mexico City, studied the paintings and estimated that they were about 6,000 years old. Alongside the many hands, there are depictions of remnants of adobe walls and of restos de fogones, remains of hearths, and small bundles of fibers, and snakes, and more.

Detail of the Cave of the Small Hands

Hands and stick-like figures. And? Could the cave of the Small Hands still hold languages, recorded on the rocks? For a moment, H hears the sounds that once reverberated from these walls; he imagines that he sees the hands as they move on the rocks. Words come to him in French, Les traces graphiques, même sonores, n'existent-elles pas toujours quelque part dans l'univers? One day, might AI, with complete coherency in another dimension, retrieve the language of the hands, or even audio fragments from the walls? Presently, we are here, too, H says to himself, with patient guides, more like welcoming hosts, sharing their land.

The visitors linger on until the sun is low and the earth is overheated; all agree that it is time to start the trek back. They walk to the nearby ladders.

From lower on the first ladder, Q calls out to H, "What will you write about the people in this cave, H?"

Head throbbing, H turns, looks down, "Agile hands, Q, ready to catch fish — swimming beneath, in the waters of the rock veins, en las aguas de las piedras," he says in Spanish.

"Keep a grip on your rung, H!" Q shoots back. And from above, still within arm's reach of H, José extends a hand to him, thinking that he's in trouble.

Days later, back in his hotel room in Oaxaca, H recalls — of all that might be remembered of the trip with Q, M and C — the visit to La Cueva de Las Manitas and the moments spent in that place of magic. Since the mid-1960s, H had not been in a cave. Barely out of their teens, H and a loved one, lost now, had picked their way through the original chambers of La Cueva de Altamira on the outskirts of the Cantabrian town of Santillana del Mar in Northern Spain. Except for an old man with a dim, flickering electric lamp, they were alone among the extraordinary animal rock paintings — bison, horses, boar, deer, mammoths, and painted hands. Replicas of Altamira — curated reproductions in the National Archeological Museum in Madrid and in Santillana del Mar, close to the actual cave — were not yet conceived. Then, in those years, the Cave of Altamira was wild, free and sheltering, as La Cueva de Las Manitas in the state of Oaxaca is today.

It's late afternoon; H decides to walk to the Zócalo and have lunch at El Asador Vasco. Though less hot than Cuicatlán, Oaxaca is still uncomfortably warm. H is spurred on to make the walk by thoughts of his usual table on the high balcony, with a cool breeze reaching him through the plaza's Indian Laurel trees. And there's the company of the Zócalo's intense life, nearby.

ALTAR OF DAY OF THE DEAD, OFFERINGS FOR LOVED ONES

H climbs the steep, uneven marble stairs of El Asador. Although he has been up and down these steps since the restaurant opened in 1978, he always forgets to count exactly how many there are. He experiences the same sense of anticipation: he knows that the same aromas, servers, white linen draped tables, and favorite menu will not have changed.

But this time, from the stairwell into the dining room, H is stopped in his tracks by a black and white photo which is attached to the altar of El Día de Muertos; the photograph is of a young man, strong arms crossed over an executive chef's coat; he's with others — family and honored employees of the restaurant— all dead, wandering souls in search of their way back home: almas errantes que buscan el camino de su hogar. Nourishing foods and quenching drinks adorn the altar. And rich earthly aromas from Oaxaca's hearths will guide them safely home again to awaiting loved ones. These are the days, at the end of October and beginning of November, when Oaxaca remembers and celebrates its dead: Los usos y costumbres de estas tierras se encuentran con el cristianismo — the indigenous vision of the world meets that of Christianity.

H says "thank you" to Arcadio Alcázar Fuentes, to his confident smile, still warm in the photo. On the days after he was murdered, all the media of the capital described him with almost identical words: "...un gran ser humano, amigo, compañero, chef... siempre preocupado por el bienestar de todos que lo rodeaban."... a grand human being, friend, companion, chef... always concerned for the wellbeing of those by his side. Other accounts of Arcadio tell of his work with the young of the city and of the time he spent teaching them.

Only one day after Arcadio's death, A and J told H of this tragedy: on April 26, 2022, two men on motorcycles gunned down Arcadio and his wife, close to the family's home. Arcadio's wife, though wounded, survived the attack. Arcadio's mother, Justina Fuentes, a well-known Oaxacan artist (as was his deceased father, Juan Alcázar, founder of the Museum of Oaxacan Painters) asked for "justicia, y aparte de justicia, que no pasara a nadie esto que estoy pasando yo. Porque es difícil, yo creo que ya basta de tanta violencia en este país."... justice, and apart from justice, may what's happening to me not happen to anyone else, because it's difficult. Enough is enough of so much violence in this country.

The Day of the Dead, H thinks is about individual loved ones—naming them—and the deference due to each.

H decides to continue his evening walk around the Zócalo and not eat anything after all. Another time, he'll return to say hello to D and to the others who serve in El Asador; he'll ask for Arcadio and his family.

Low-spirited, H shuffles around the kiosque of the Zócalo until dusk. Next morning in his hotel's green patio, over a cup of coffee and in the presence of familiar faces, he's a little less downcast. One long-time hotel guest asks him about his plans for the coming weeks; he remembers that he and Q will soon see several of their old friends at the grand opening of R's mask exhibition in CaSa, San Agustín Etla. He smiles, in spite of himself, at the idea of this coming event. Months earlier, when H thought that he might see R and K, his friends missed the opening for the work of Selma Guisande and the photographs of Muybridge. Days before the opening, R had been attacked by black wasps and had suffered pain and swelling for days. H first learned of this bizarre attack in an overheard conversation that evening at the Centro.

H and R Stand Before R's Mexican Masks

MEXICAN DANCES AND MASKS: VISITS TO RENÉ BUSTAMANTE

On a hot afternoon in mid-December, H and R stand before some of R's Mexican masks. Vitrines and walls of masks fill the expansive gallery of El Centro de las Artes de San Agustín (CaSa), in San Agustín Etla. Opened in 2006, this art center is a wonder of regenesis — from a 19th century industrial factory to a Oaxacan artist's (Juchitán's Francisco Toledo) conception of a place of international and national creative inclusivity. CaSa's buildings sit high, looking out on the towering beauty of the mountains of the Sierra Madre de Oaxaca. The small town of San Agustín Etla, north of Oaxaca city, is less than an hour's drive from the capital.

Weeks earlier, R wrote to H, describing the work going into his exhibition, Timeless Faces: Evolution and Permanence of Mexican Dances and Masks: "Hola, H, so good that the time you are coming is near. Yes, you will see the show.... On November 12th, I will start moving masks for the enormous show that will open December 16th in the big hall of CaSa... I am trying to finish the photos and texts for the catalogue so, yes, busy as never before in my entire life, but we have much to talk about."

Now, H and R are together again in another mask exhibit in which R shares some of his enormous collection — hundreds of masks gathered over decades from around the world with the eye of a cultural anthropologist. On such occasions, strangers, friends, and reporters always press R:

They have urgent questions. H can hear some of R's steady and polite responses:

"Yes, of course, you're right to ask about the mask and its sinister reputation in the West. But this is not the case with these masks. They often tell a story, a story of a character in a community."

From even deeper in the pressing crowd, another question, followed by R's response, "...the devil mask dancing... presenting problems, grievances that neighbors may have, all while dancing in public... a form of communal therapy."

Then leaning closer, voice lowered, R says, "I'm getting tired, H, even among friends. So many questions. So many of the same questions."

And R answers another question, "I see the dances of the masks as a part of our history... from a time long ago, before the Conquest."

There are more questions to follow. H doesn't have a chance to respond to R, to commiserate with him. Instead, he glances over his left shoulder at the grinning monkey mask behind the glass: It will be up to the monkey mask to play its role with the onlooking crowd, H thinks. He will surely exercise some control over the crowd's exuberance. Yet, alas, it is unlikely that the monkey mask in Oaxaca plays the role assumed by this mask in West Africa. But it could be.

R's Home, the Dogon Satimbe Mask and Mythic Treachery

H's visit to R and K's mountain home follows some days after the mask exhibition at CaSa. With the warmest of welcomes at the main gate, R and K guide C, M, Q and H towards the front door. And then, over a richly set table of local garden vegetables and Oaxaca's cheeses, their conversation turns to travels, friends, books and masks.

Later, after sips of a mezcal made by a neighbor, they stroll in R's garden of a hundred different Oaxacan cacti and succulents. Stopping, H turns to R, "Seeing all your Mexican masks at CaSa made me think of our collections of African masks, R. Do you have a favorite mask from Mali, from the months that you walked in Africa?"

"That's so difficult.... But yes, if I were to choose just one, the Satimbe." R and H return inside to one of the smaller rooms of his remarkable home. R built the home with Cantera and river stones and adobe bricks made on his property; it has high vaulted ceilings and long, thick Ocote pine beams. "...materials that I have always loved," R says. "I learned what I know about using these materials by attending the classes of a colleague and friend at UC Berkeley while I was teaching there. He let me sit in on his architecture course."

In the photo, R stands in front of a collection of mostly Malian masks—his dark silver hair just below the Dogon Satimbe mask. The story of this mask is one of H's favorites: The female figure mounted above the mask's box is named Yasigine; her arms reach out and upward to the sky, towards Ama, one of the Dogon dieties associated with rain and goodness. In Dogon country, the Satimbe mask is the only female representation allowed in the otherwise all male Dogon secret society of masks; this is a society with its own secret language. Mamadou, a dear Dogon friend, talked to H about these things while they walked together in le Pays Dogon. The Dogon believe that Satimbe is a sister and among the first masks. Long ago, before the time of the masks, a woman found her in a field near the village of Youga Dogorou. The woman put the mask on and danced—to the attendant admiration of her people. Seeing the power that the mask had, the woman's husband stole Satimbe. An act of mythic treachery, H thinks.

While still in the cool of this small room, R and H talk about their long walks in Africa. H remembers the footpaths of the Dogon Country, on the heights of the steep sandstone cliff, home to the diverse Dogon people. Although R and H walked separately, on different paths, they share stories of watching the dancing masks, years ago. The energy of being close to the masks, can still be felt now in Oaxaca.

That evening, H will return to his hotel and reread what R wrote—almost thirty years before in the catalogue of his African mask collection for an exhibition in Oaxaca: "Jamás debe considerarse bella o fea una máscara, cuando ésta se encuentra separada del danzante y del baile; no fue concebida para apreciarse en reposo. La máscara es teatro, drama, vida, espíritu y rito. Una figura cuyos brazos se elevan hacia el cielo tiene un significado trascendente en una tierra que carece de lluvia y de presas de agua." "A mask should never be considered beautiful or ugly when it is separated from the dancer and the dance; it was not conceived to be appreciated at rest. The mask is theater, drama, life, spirit and ritual. A figure whose arms are raised towards the sky has a transcendent meaning in a land that lacks rain and reservoirs." Although maybe not writing with the Satimbe mask specifically in mind, R captures, from afar, the critical importance of place when presenting masks. R writes while near the surrounding indigenous cultures of Oaxaca and close to the Afro-Mexican communities of La Costa Chica, the long Oaxacan littoral on the Pacific Ocean. In R's company, H feels that Oaxaca is a crucible of powerful sensibilities, a natural place for the appreciation of the world's diversity.

Friendship: R & H & the Artist Rick Bartow

R has many Rick Bartow paintings and drawings in his home. They were close friends, the North American of indigenous Yurok ancestry and R, whose family members came from Europe in the sixteenth century. "We shared much in common, Bartow and I," R says. "...our love and obsession with masks, painting, creative process, other cultures, going for long walks in the forest or on the Oregon-Newport coast. Or just cooking..."

Rick Bartow's people, the Yurok, live today in and around the coastal area of the Klamath River. From his decades in Northern California, H remembers that they are one of the largest tribes there and are well-known as storytellers, carvers of redwood canoes, deer and elk hunters, and salmon river fishermen. The Yurok are also revitalizing their language in the towns and small settlements of Humboldt and Del Norte Counties.

During every visit to R's home, H stops in front of his favorite Bartow work. In the photo on the left, he and R are seated before a painting of a coyote or wolf creature. It is the raw, dark energy of this animal against a red background that holds H's attention. He could imagine this wounded figure as a spiritual link between the Native Peoples of the U.S. Northwest and of Canada and of those of Mexico.

In an earlier exhibit catalog, R describes the subject matter of a large number of Bartow's works as being like "an Indigenous totem in the Pacific Northwest forest, where it appears to us as a reminder of the presence of ancestral spirits." Seeing this painting, H feels Bartow's empathy with an injured, tortured being. A personal anguish on the artist's part? Perhaps, but also an expressed oneness with nature, an indigenous, ageless view of our world.

While still lingering in R and K's home, H emails this photo to his American-Chilean colleague in Northern California at Cal Poly Humboldt. And, in the strangest twist of events, H's colleague answers straight back, "H, truly incredible... I'm hanging a Rick Bartow work on my office wall, this very minute."

A Gift for Aunt Chona: Oaxaca & Beyond, H Leaves Oaxaca

In the early morning hours of his last day in Oaxaca, on his way to the airport, H receives a message from J, "Hola H, estuve recientemente en Valerio Trujano y entregué a Tía Chona el libro que le enviaste."

"Hello H, I was recently in Valerio Trujano and I delivered to Aunt Chona the book that you sent her."

"Hola, J, ¡Qué maravilla de foto! Gracias por haber pensado en mandarme algo tan apreciado."

"What a wonderful photo! Thank you for thinking of sending me something so appreciated."

Seeing the photo brings joy to H's heart. Aunt Chona and many of her family members are seated close to the arches of Valerio Trujano's aqueduct. Now, he looks forward to sharing this moment with others, editors and writers, who were a part of the book that is in the hands of Tía Chona.

H has said his long goodbyes to his friends. He is by himself, leaving, still not knowing if the Mexican version of the anthology has appeared locally. After a sojourn of months, he is headed home. He'll soon see loved ones.

On the plane, leather satchel stowed near his feet, he thinks about his notebooks—filled with scribblings, erasures, and photo captions. The writing project that he has been working on these months while in Oaxaca is on his mind—a short novel, titled, OAXACA Stories Along The Way. His plan is to finish it while spending a few months back in Northern California or Southern Oregon—to stay there until this novella is published and on the shelves of bookstores. Being in the U. S. will be fine, for a while.

EPILOGUE

View the world of a local photographer... a market vendor... a painter... an academic... all through the eyes of an author who has fallen in love. This is not the simple infatuation of fairy tales, but the real love that comes from appreciating the whole. It comes from the beauty of a city and the hearts of its populace, but also in the conflict of visitor and resident, city and rural, race and gender, privilege and poverty, capitalism and culture. In those conflicts and harmonies, miseries and dreams, comes the true soul of a place, a resilience reflected in the people who come together to forge the relationships and history that make Oaxaca such a singular place.

The book opens at an exhibit, the conversations filtering through the thoughts and senses of our guide. Back at his hotel, then out in the streets, the scenes unfold: food, literature, visual arts, public spaces, conversations, nature, and musings fill the spaces of the book's canvas. The past, the future, and the moment come together through the author's interpretations, orienting the pieces until we arrive at both a singular perspective and panoramic view.

All writings come with intention, with an inextricable pull for a narrative plot. But this author resists the temptation in lieu of creating true oases of experience, the story scenes only existing in the appreciation of the moment, or at least in the impression of moments through the author's curious gaze and fallible memory. Bias is implicit, but by recognizing it and embracing it within the context of marvel, the reader too marvels at the small filtered moments of city life.

The author identifies the people with letters of the alphabet, each treated with equal deference and respect. Of note is the absence of the letter "I," because this is not a story that centers "I," but the people themselves, the connection among them, and the strands that magically weave them into a city-wide whole. H emerges as the constant throughout, though not as a central character, but as the central receiver of sensory experience, culture, ideas, and history. Where the author reveals his story, he is not focusing himself, but the honest conversations of equal participants, centering the relationships between H and his Oaxacan counterparts.

Throughout, H calls into question his own ego, history, and any ulterior motive in order to find "the real" Mexico beyond the prefabricated cultural stereotypes. To move beyond the coopted Oaxaca of outsiders, H becomes a temporary resident and lets Oaxaca come to him on its own terms. He opens himself up to be changed in the process, allowing "...the intensity of the creative spirit of Oaxaca [to mold] habits and obsessions to its own time..."

The book's text and visual snapshots follow their own course, revealing the artist circles where H socializes, but also those intersecting worlds in the local neighborhoods and areas beyond the city. Oaxaca delivers unlimited opportunities for his creative explorations, "a crucible of powerful sensibilities, a natural place for the appreciation of the world's diversity." Letters and stories from distant lands intrude, though they do not distract from this story of Oaxaca, they are instead foils for a deeper understanding of the disparate realities and relationships of this complex multi-cultural city.

One can never write the empirical story, the never-changing story; one can only write the story of one's relationships with a person, place, or object at a particular moment in time. As those relationships build upon one another, they create an impression upon which the depth of the environment comes into focus. The only question for the author is when to stop. When does he feel he has seen into the soul of it? When is there enough of a picture for a reader to get a sense of it? There are infinite moments, infinite stories and images, infinite relationships to choose from; one story can never hope to capture them all. Always there is more left unsaid, more left to be discovered, questions left unanswered–as is rarely true in artificial narratives, yet is always true in life. Thank you, dear H, for defining the time and place as honestly as you have, translating that world through your gaze, and projecting an indelible image behind my closed eyes.

Kyle Morgan
Arcata, California

ACKNOWLEDGEMENTS

Dear Readers,

The existence of this novella, Oaxaca Stories Along The Way, is in large part thanks to the creative vision of the University Library at Cal Poly Humboldt. I owe a debt of gratitude to Cyril Oberlander, Dean of the University Library, Kyle Morgan, Librarian for The Press at Cal Poly Humboldt, and to Wilder Yaconelli, who is completing a student internship at The Press at Cal Poly Humboldt. In these fraught times, the library's light from the hill, from the promontory overlooking the Pacific Ocean, continues to shine on a diverse community of students, staff, faculty and on the peoples of Northern California.

I also wish to thank those who work in the Public Library of Ashland, Oregon, especially, Ryan Murphy, for his patience in helping me format my writing and edit my photographs. Ashland Library of Jackson County is a welcoming place, welcoming all in this small town.

Dorothy M. Pendleton proofread and suggested edits at every turning of a page. Still, I'm now obliged to accept sole responsibility for my errors.

Finally, to friends and colleagues in Oaxaca de Juárez, Oaxaca, Mexico, and to those in Arcata, California, I carry you with me; you, too, are always near.

James E. Gaasch